Town and Country in Early-Medieval Bavaria

Two studies in urban and comital structure

Carl I. Hammer

BAR International Series 2437
2012

Published in 2016 by
BAR Publishing, Oxford

BAR International Series 2437

Town and Country in Early-Medieval Bavaria

ISBN 978 1 4073 1036 7

© C I Hammer and the Publisher 2012

COVER IMAGE *Bavarian Central State Archives (Hauptstaatsarchiv), Munich, Jesuitenorden, Kolleg München, Urkunden Ebersberg 1: Charter of King Arnolf for Sigihard, 1 January 888. See pages 27 and 39.*

The author's moral rights under the 1988 UK Copyright,
Designs and Patents Act are hereby expressly asserted.

All rights reserved. No part of this work may be copied, reproduced, stored,
sold, distributed, scanned, saved in any form of digital format or transmitted
in any form digitally, without the written permission of the Publisher.

BAR Publishing is the trading name of British Archaeological Reports (Oxford) Ltd.
British Archaeological Reports was first incorporated in 1974 to publish the BAR
Series, International and British. In 1992 Hadrian Books Ltd became part of the BAR
group. This volume was originally published by Archaeopress in conjunction with
British Archaeological Reports (Oxford) Ltd / Hadrian Books Ltd, the Series principal
publisher, in 2012. This present volume is published by BAR Publishing, 2016.

Printed in England

BAR titles are available from:

        BAR Publishing
        122 Banbury Rd, Oxford, OX2 7BP, UK
EMAIL   info@barpublishing.com
PHONE +44 (0)1865 310431
  FAX   +44 (0)1865 316916
        www.barpublishing.com

Table of Contents

Table of Contents. i

Preface iii

Introduction. 1

Part I. Borough and Marketplace: Proto- and Para-urbanism in Early-Medieval Bavaria

I.1 Early-Medieval Bavaria, An Urban Backwater? 11

I.2 Proto-Urbanism 12

I.3 Para-Urbanism 18

I.4 A Two-Tiered Urban Landscape 24

Part II. From Sheriff to Count: Comital Government and the "Feudal Transformation" in Bavaria

Comital Structures and Personnel in Carolingian Bavaria

II.1 Early Carolingian Comital Rule: The Regime of Audulf 27

II.2 The Later Carolingians 30

II.3 Carolingian Conclusions and Ottonian Outlook 33

Bavaria's First Count and the "Feudal Transformation"

II.4 Abbot Williram's "Chronicle" of Ebersberg 34

II.5 Sigihard's Origins 35

II.6 Sigihard's Descendants in Ebersberg 38

II.7 Sigihard and the "Feudal Transformation" 39

II.8 Epilogue 43

Bibliography

A. Primary Sources 47

B. Secondary Sources 48

Figures and Exhibits

Sketch-Map of Boroughs and Marketplaces in Early-Medieval Bavaria 53

City Plan of Early-Medieval Regensburg 54

Exhibit I.1: Proto-Urbanism in Early-Medieval Bavaria before *ca* 1000 55

Exhibit I.2: Civic Organization and Tenements in Regensburg and Passau 56

Exhibit I.3: Raffelstetten Inquest Concerning Tolls, 903x6 57

Exhibit I.4: Bavarian Trade Along the Danube River as Described in the Raffelstetten Inquest 59

Exhibit II.1: Documents on the Carolingian *Comes* in Bavaria... 60

Exhibit II.2: Dated Official Spans for Senior Laymen Attending Bavarian Missatical Courts............. 61

Exhibit II.3: Comital Spans in Late-Carolingian Western Bavaria.. 62

Exhibit II.4: The *Chronicle of Ebersberg* Written under Abbot Williram 63

Exhibit II.5: Genealogy of the Ebersbergers.. 65

Preface

These studies began as papers for conferences of medievalists. Part One, "Borough and Marketplace", was read at the Thirty-Sixth Annual Sewanee Medieval Colloquium in 2009. The scope of my Sewanee paper was essentially the same as that printed here, but because of severe time constraints it could only be presented in highly condensed form there. I have since revised certain portions. The first section of Part Two, "From Sheriff to Count", on the comital structure of Carolingian Bavaria, was prepared for the Forty-First International Congress on Medieval Studies at Kalamazoo in 2006. My intention always was to extend that prosopographical study of 9th century Carolingian sheriffs into the 10th century and to examine the developments which ultimately led to the establishment of feudal counts and their lordships in Bavaria. That is what I have done now in the second section but only as a kind of "trial trench". There I have "excavated" what I believe to be the first Bavarian comital dynasty, the Ebersbergers. They are a well-known family and have been the subject of several excellent studies which I have used extensively and cite with gratitude. But I think the approach and particularly the context here are original.

My first intention was to publish these two Parts as separate journal articles, but I then came to think that they were in several ways complementary and would benefit from being read together in a short monograph. Indeed, a late-Carolingian comital official, Sigihard, plays an important role in both Parts. I am particularly grateful that Dr David Davison of BAR agreed so readily and so helpfully. At a more general level, these two studies deal with the earliest history of two parallel institutions, the development of the urban "borough" and the emergence of castle-based lordships within the comital organization of the countryside, which formed the twin bases for the estate-based feudal constitution of the high Middle Ages.[1] Although the two Parts can be read independently, I have tried to make them consistent and to reduce repetition. Cross-references have been added where this seemed helpful. The addition of a full, unified Bibliography should assist anyone who wishes to study these matters further.

I also realize that the history of Bavaria is unfamiliar to most people and even to professional medievalists. Accordingly, I have tried to provide the necessary historical background for both Parts in the Introduction where I have also taken the opportunity to explore an historical problem, the nature of the early-medieval "state". This issue is not only of interest to medievalists. As will be seen, it is also a part of modern Bavarian political identity.

As a person whose career has been in business, not academe, it is a particular social as well as intellectual pleasure for me to participate in academic conferences, particularly ones as intimate and congenial as Sewanee. Those attending my presentations are seldom experts on the topic, but their friendly questions and interest are both an encouragement to me and a challenge to clarify my thinking. In separate communications, several experts have kindly offered their detailed and always helpful criticisms of my various drafts. As one who lives and works outside the normal academic networks, I particularly value such friendly personal contacts with people whose scholarship I respect – even when I disagree (as, at times, I do). Professor Michael Mitterauer, formerly head of the Institute for Economic and Social History at the University of Vienna, provided his comments on the first Part, a topic which he knows better than anyone else. An anonymous early academic Reader supplied numerous criticisms of the second Part which all have been taken into account where needed. Professor Chris Wickham of Oxford, as Reader for BAR, offered his always valuable observations and drew my attention to some recent scholarship of which I was unaware. Professor Michael McCormick (Harvard) also gave me welcome encouragement on Part One. My neighbor, the political scientist Professor Michael Goodhart (University of Pittsburgh), read through the Introduction from the perspective of his

---

[1] See now the wide-ranging exposition in Michael Mitterauer's, *Warum Europa? Mittelalterliche Grundlagen eines Sonderweges*, Chapter 4, esp. pp. 127-31 (English translation: *Why Europe?*, pp. 118-23), here with regard to aristocratic castles, p. 131/122: "The new direction taken by fortification practice (*Befestigungswesen*) in western Europe from the late Carolingian period was a totally unique development. Alongside the classic walled town, the lord's castle now emerged as a new type of military installation (*Wehranlage*)."

discipline. The Department of the History of Art and Architecture at the University of Pittsburgh has generously continued to appoint me as a Research Associate over several years; without such status it would be quite impossible for me as a private person to obtain the research materials I need – especially now when so much is available only by extraordinarily restrictive and expensive electronic means. My wife, Jóna, fondly known to her former Duquesne University colleagues as "Jóna the knife" for her ruthless editorial skills, took the immense and tedious trouble to copy-read all of the text without dismembering it. She has provided me with generous and ungrudging support for many years since I retired myself from a remunerative career in international business and took up (unremunerative) medieval history again.

Introduction: Early-Medieval Bavaria, a Precocious State?

On 6 February 806 the Emperor Charlemagne published a prospective division of his empire amongst his three sons by his wife Hildegard.[1] In the second article or chapter there he assigned to the second oldest, Pippin, now a king in Italy: "Bavaria as Tassilo held it except for two estates of which the names are Ingolstadt and Lauterhofen, which we formerly granted to Tassilo as benefices and which pertain to the district which is called the Nordgau", which district Charlemagne then granted in its entirety to his older son, Karl.[2] Charlemagne's grant to Pippin of Bavaria and of additional territories to the west in Alemannia restored, perhaps consciously, the ancient unity of the Roman administrative diocese of *Italia Annonaria* which had joined the provinces of northern Italy with transalpine *Raetia Prima* and *Secunda*, now the duchies of Chur and Bavaria. To these Charlemagne added the ancient provinces of *Noricum Ripense* and *Mediterraneanum* which straddled the Alps immediately to the east of *Raetia*. Under the Late Empire, *Noricum* had been part of the separate diocese of *Illyricum*, but it had been united ecclesiastically with eastern *Raetia Secunda* under the patriarchate of Aquileia after the decline of Milan in the fifth century.[3] *Noricum* now was also a part of Bavaria, "as Tassilo held it".

Tassilo was Charlemagne's first cousin whom he had deposed as duke of the Bavarians in 788 and finally condemned for treasonous activities at the council of Frankfurt in 794 where Tassilo renounced all claims in Bavaria. Whether Tassilo had ever, in fact, "held" (*tenuit*) Bavaria from Charlemagne is open to doubt.[4] From the late 7th century under the early duke, Theodo, and his immediate descendants and then under the new (and possibly related) ducal dynasty (known as the "Agilolfings") beginning with Tassilo's father, Odilo, the Bavarian dukes had constructed a distinctive and independent ducal rule.[5] Under Tassilo, a Carolingian grandson of Charles Martell through his mother, this rule took on distinctly royal character encouraged by his consort, Liutpirc, a Langobard princess royal from neighboring Italy. Rather, Charlemagne's aggressive claim reasserted so prominently in 806 (and possibly believed) was necessary to describe the full extent of the territory which Pippin was now to rule over from his primary seat in the former Langobard kingdom of Italy. Thus, the extent of Tassilo's duchy must have been known with some precision. No doubt, after Tassilo's deposition inquests were held and surveys conducted to determine the precise value of Bavaria to the Crown.[6] The excellent *Historical Atlas of Bavaria* provides a cartographic reconstruction of the Bavarian duchy in the last year of Tassilo's rule, 788.[7] There we can see that Karl's newly-granted Nordgau with its two contentious estates, Ingolstadt and Lauterhofen, lay north of the great river Danube – and thus beyond the Roman frontier – and west

---

[1] *Divisio Regnorum*, MGH, Capitularia regum Francorum, vol. 1, Nr 45, pp. 126-30; in the event, Karl and Pippin predeceased their father, and the entire empire passed undivided to the youngest son, Ludwig whose previous rule had been based on the Aquitaine.

[2] *Divisio Regnorum*, c. 2, p. 127: "et Baiovariam, sicut Tassilo tenuit, exceptis duabus villis quarum nomina sunt Ingoldestat et Lutrahahof, quas nos quondam Tassiloni beneficiavimus et pertinent ad pagum qui dicitur Northgowe"; c. 3, p. 127: "et partem Baioariae quae dicitur Northgow".

[3] For the connections between Bavaria and Italy in the 6th and early 7th centuries see now C. Hammer, "Early Merovingian Bavaria: A Late Antique Italian Perspective". The Roman topography of *Raetia* and *Noricum* is now presented definitively in the *Barrington Atlas of the Greek and Roman World*, Maps 12, 19 and 20.

[4] The most important modern challenge to this Carolingian historical claim was Matthias Becher's 1993 *Eid und Herrschaft*, pp. 21-77, where massive doubt was cast on the ingenious indictment of Tassilo constructed by Carolingian historiography. In my opinion, however, Becher did not go quite far enough, for which see C. Hammer, "*Pippinus Rex*: Pippin's Plot of 792 and Bavaria", pp. 255-58.

[5] For the early dukes and their Bavaria see the invaluable studies in Joachim Jahn's *Ducatus Baiuvariorum. Das Bairische Herzogtum der Agilolfinger*; the development of ducal and then early royal rule in Bavaria is examined in C. Hammer, *From Ducatus to Regnum: Ruling Bavaria under the Merovingians and Early Carolingians*.

[6] A later effort of this sort is presented below, Part II.8. The 8th century property surveys carried out by major churches, most notably Salzburg, must be a reflex of such an effort to identify fiscal property, for which see H. Wolfram, *Salzburg, Bayern, Österreich*, pp. 207-12.

[7] *Bayerischer Geschichtsatlas*, Map 14a, with commentary by Gertrud Diepolder on pp. 70-71. It must be remembered that early-medieval countries had borders which were less well-delineated and more fluid than those implied by modern cartography. In particular, the effectiveness of any unified lordship would have varied widely from region to region. Thus, frontiers are better conceived as gradual changes in shading than as sharp contrasts. Nevertheless, historical maps are still essential for conceiving any territorial entities.

of the river Naab. South of the Danube, Pippin's new Bavarian lands extended from the mouth of the river Lech over the Alps to the upper course of the river Etsch/Adige and southeast to the valley of the river Drau/Drava. From the defunct episcopal seat at Neuburg just east of the Lech on the Danube to the southern bishopric of Säben above the Etsch was a straight-line distance of 250 km which could be traversed along the ancient Via Claudia across the valley of the river Inn and then over the Alps by the Reschen Pass or by the more easterly Brenner Pass, still today the primary route to Italy. The centers of Maria Saal and the Karnburg in far southeastern Carinthia lay about 350 km from Neuburg across the Alps by way of Salzburg. They were isolated Bavarian posts in the large Slavic territory now comprising ancient *Noricum Mediterraneanum* which had only been conquered by Tassilo in 772 and which could not yet have been fully annexed nor assimilated. In *Noricum Ripense* directly to the north across the mountains, the effective Bavarian frontier with the recently defeated Avars reached only to the river Enns, an alpine tributary of the Danube.

Within this very extensive country, the most intensely developed – or, rather, documented – Bavarian landscape lay north of the Alps and between the rivers Lech and Enns. This central Bavarian landscape, "Old Bavaria", was crossed by two other major alpine tributaries of the Danube, the Isar and the Inn with its own tributary, the Salzach, all of which had significant settlement along their river valleys. In addition to Säben, Bavaria contained four bishoprics, Freising, Regensburg, Passau and Salzburg, and numerous monasteries and ducal estates.[8] The *Historical Atlas* also shows that two centuries later this basic geographical configuration was, with three exceptions, essentially unchanged.[9] The Nordgau with the Bonifacian bishopric of Eichstätt on its western border was now an integral part of Bavaria, and Bavarian lordship now extended south of the Danube far to the east of the river Enns and even beyond the ancient Pannonian frontier: the East March. To the southeast, Carinthia between the rivers Drau and Mur now had numerous documented centers of authority and economic activity which, in many cases, like those of the East March, were connected to lordships in "Old Bavaria".

These two historical maps set the geographical and temporal limits to the following study which will examine two essential structures of the economy and governmental authority in the 9th and 10th centuries. But, before we begin, I want to explore briefly the wider context in which these structures developed over the two early-medieval centuries under consideration. By looking at the maps with their multitude of symbols in various colors, one could easily conclude that Bavaria was merely a geographical agglomeration of numerous and discrete "local societies" as a highly-detailed recent study is titled.[10] This characterization has a certain justification. The servile populations of the many dependent manors and villages were, no doubt, preoccupied with themselves, their families and their purely local village and seigneurial concerns.[11] Likewise, the Bavarian aristocracy, despite its surprisingly wide-ranging connections which reached from Francia and Alemannia in the west into Italy in the south and Slavic lands in the east, was also divided into numerous regional groupings with their own social solidarities and local loyalties.[12] The most important of these divisions was the growing split between western Old Bavaria and the frontier lands to the east and southeast which led to the creation of separate Duchy of Carinthia in 976 and the installation of a new and increasingly-autonomous dynasty, the Babenbergers, in the East March beyond the river Enns in that same year. Thus, in many respects, early-medieval Bavaria was a highly fragmented polity. But what strikes me much more forcefully – and which the two maps reveal so strikingly – is Bavaria's persistent and tenacious unity from the late 8th to the late 10th century.

---

[8] There is a convenient exposition of these early "central places" with maps in K. Fehn, *Die zentralörtliche Funktionen früher Zentren in Altbayern.*

[9] *Bayerischer Geschichtsatlas*, Map 15, with commentary by Gertrud Diepolder on pp. 71-72.

[10] T. Kohl, *Lokale Gesellschaften. Formen der Gemeinschaft in Bayern vom 8. bis zum 10. Jahrhundert.*

[11] See C. Hammer, *A Large-Scale Slave Society of the Early Middle Ages*, esp. pp. 26-34, with literature cited there.

[12] For example, my own micro-regional studies in C. Hammer, "The Social Landscape of the Prague Sacramentary", esp. pp. 53-64; *idem*, "'Crowding the King': Rebellion and Political Violence in Late-Carolingian Bavaria and Italy", esp. pp. 500-05; *idem*, *From Ducatus to Regnum*, Excursus 3: "In Search of *Awigozeshusir*", pp. 305-25; and *idem*, "Hoc and Hnaef in Bavaria?", with map on p. 50; all with references to other relevant secondary literature.

The official website of the Bavarian government (www.bayern.de) states proudly that, "Bavaria is one of the oldest states in Europe. Its origins go back to the 6th century AD", evidently to the "Origins of the Duchy of Bavaria" in that century which is the first event cited in the officially-endorsed chronology of Bavarian history displayed there.[13] At first sight this is an odd claim, since the early-medieval duchy of Bavaria and the modern federal state are hardly coterminous. By the 8th century, as we saw, Bavaria's territory extended south and east to include all of modern Austria and portions of modern Italy and Slovenia. However, Tassilo's duchy did not include the modern Bavarian administrative districts of Swabia and of Franconia west of the Lech and north of the Danube. Still, the modern Bavarian administrative districts of Upper and Lower Bavaria and the Upper Palatinate encompass much of the settled core of early-medieval Old Bavaria with three of its five episcopal seats while omitting some adjacent regions in Austria, particularly in the federal states of Salzburg, Upper Austria, and Tyrol which, of course, can also claim Bavarian descent! We must also make some adjustment to the Bavarian government's overly enthusiastic chronology. While it is quite certain that in the mid-to-late 6th century some peoples known to outsiders as "Bavarians" lived somewhere in the vicinity of modern Bavaria and that the Franks established a duchy at this time to secure their frontier with Langobard Italy, there is no reason to conflate the two into an ethnic "Dukedom of Bavaria"; on the contrary, it is quite unlikely.[14]

But, in my view, these are relatively minor and obvious quibbles and easily resolved. By far the deeper and richer historical problem arises from the Bavarian government's clear implication that its early-medieval predecessor – however large or ancient it may have been – was a "state". Any medieval historian will immediately recognize such a bold claim as highly contentious. Indeed, the eminent American medievalist, the late Professor Joseph Strayer, in an essay still cited regularly and with respect, asserts quite clearly that England and France were the first European states to emerge and then only between the 1100 and 1300.[15] Moreover, as Strayer himself clearly recognized, the term "state", with its modern ideological and organizational connotations, can only be applied with qualification to any medieval polity. German-language historians, with their particular research traditions and political experience, have been amongst the most reluctant to do so fearing, correctly, the risk of anachronism or worse. And, yet, this issue continues to attract serious historical attention.[16] Is it then possible that Bavaria may, in fact, be "one of the oldest states in Europe" as the Munich politicians but not the Princeton Professor think? As Charlemagne's attempted disposition of his great empire demonstrates, by the later 8th century Bavaria was clearly an important polity under the authority of a significant, albeit unwelcome ruler. Was it then also a "state" or, if not, did one emerge during the following two centuries?

This may seem to be merely a definitional problem – as, in part, it surely is. Walter Pohl has drawn attention to a simple modern definition of "state" which was incorporated into the Montevideo Convention of 1933.[17] There, for a polity to be recognized as a person in international law, that is, as

---

[13] Oddly (to me), this chronological table then jumps over nearly six centuries of Bavarian history (more than one-third of the total!) to the foundation of Munich in 1158 which is at the outer limits of the urban developments we shall consider in Part I. Thus, all of the period presented here and comprising the first volume of the *Handbuch der bayerischen Geschichte* is excluded from current official Bavarian historical consciousness, and the older Bavarian ducal dynasties of the Agilolfings and the Luitpoldings, the darlings of earlier Bavarian nationalists, are laid under a "damnatio memoriae" in favor of the much later Welfs and Wittelsbachs! The current unimportance of the early Middle Ages for Bavarian history is also reflected by its very low priority in the Bavarian National Library's large on-line reference project: www.historisches-lexikon-bayerns.de.
[14] The evidence is examined critically in C. Hammer, "Early Merovingian Bavaria: A Late-Antique Italian Perspective". In March 2011 the Institute for Bavarian History in Munich sponsored a conference on Bavarian origins. Summaries of the papers, many archaeological, can be read at: Tagungsbericht *Von Raetien und Noricum zur frühmittelalterlichen Baiuvaria*. 14.-16.03.2010, Benediktbeuern, in H-Soz-u-Kult, 08.07.2010 (<http://hsozkult.geschichte.hu-berlin.de/tagungsberichte/id=3176>); publication of the proceedings is planned.
[15] J. Strayer, *On the Medieval Origins of the Modern State*, p. vi: "The first European states that have endured to our own time were formed in France and England, and all other European states were strongly influenced by the example of these precursors", with the discussion beginning at p. 36.
[16] See the two recent volumes of essays from a major research project and conferences held at the Institute for Medieval Research in Vienna: *Staat im frühen Mittelalter* (2006), and *Der frühmittelalterliche Staat – europäische Perspektiven* (2009). Very useful general discussions are provided in the earlier volume by W. Pohl, "Staat und Herrschaft im Frühmittelalter" and by P. Wormald, "Pre-modern 'State' and 'Nation'"; and in the later volume by R. Schieffer, "Die internationale Forschung zur Staatlichkeit in der Karolingerzeit".
[17] W. Pohl, "Staat und Herrschaft im Frühmittelalter", p. 10.

a "state", it must possess four qualifications: 1. a permanent population; 2. a defined territory; 3. a government; and, 4. the capacity to enter into relations with other states (a qualification not mentioned by Pohl). By this definition there can be little doubt that Tassilo's duchy of Bavaria in the late 8th century was, indeed, a "state" even though his ability to enter into relations with other "states", in this case, with the Langobards and the Avars, was contested vigorously by Charlemagne and served as strong grounds for Tassilo's condemnation. But it is immediately evident that this modern definition – which, of course, was not constructed with our concerns in mind – leaves vital historical questions open. Most obviously, what do we mean by "a government"? It is hardly likely that Tassilo exercised a "monopoly of coercive power" (*Gewaltmonopol*) in his Bavaria, a characteristic which has dominated much of the modern German discussion on this topic.[18] For myself, as an Anglophone who, in Professor Rudolf Schieffer's words, takes, "a rather easy-going approach to terminological issues", I am more inclined to Patrick Wormald's argument that we should, "start out from what pre-modern polities can be shown to have done, and only then, consider the label we can best affix to them".[19] Thus, I propose to take an empirical approach here and to offer a brief historical review of some items which seem to me to have promoted (or retarded) Bavarian "stateliness" (*Staatlichkeit*) before returning to the larger question of early-medieval Bavaria's political status.[20] This will be a highly unusual undertaking because studies of the early-medieval state invariably concern themselves with the rather larger entity which later became Germany (at some point) rather than with its various historical parts.

But first it is necessary to specify who and what is not included in the following discussion, since the political community which comprised the Bavarian polity and the whole population living within Bavaria were not identical. Even though this issue is not essential to the Montevideo definition, it must be of interest to historians who, nevertheless, often neglect it. Who, then, was part of the "political community" which comprised this putative Bavarian "state"? In the first place, probably the vast majority of the entire population should be excluded because of their complete servility or otherwise unfree and dependent status. These persons were under the essentially unlimited seigneurial authority of their masters and participated in public life either not at all or only very rarely during our period, for example, as agents and legal witnesses to their masters' business. The apparent exceptions to this rule, that is, dependents who were raised by their masters to responsible positions, in fact, prove it, since much of their usefulness derived from their complete dependency. These privileged dependents included the later "ministerials", the so-called "serf-knights", who were given important administrative and, later, military responsibilities by their masters and who become quite numerous towards the end of our period. Their relatively-privileged status enabled marriages with free women which, nevertheless, created severe legal disabilities for their offspring and, occasionally, for their spouses.[21] They could advise and otherwise influence their masters but not act independently on their own behalf.

Likewise, about half of the entire population, that is, women, should be excluded. It is true that aristocratic women could exercise significant political influence through their husbands and other male

---

[18] R. Schieffer, "Die internationale Forschung zur Staatlichkeit in der Karolingerzeit", pp. 44-46.

[19] R. Schieffer, "Die internationale Forschung zur Staatlichkeit in der Karolingerzeit", p. 49: "in der neueren anglophonen Literatur ... scheint mir jedenfalls ein recht gelassener Umgang mit dieser terminologischen Frage vorzuherrschen." P. Wormald, "Pre-modern 'State' and 'Nation'", p. 17; Chris Wickham, who is more rigorous theoretically than most early-medievalists, still remarks that, "if the concept [i. e. definition of the state] is seen as an ideal type ... there is no 'right characterization, only more – or less – useful ones" (*Framing the Early Middle Ages*, p. 57, fn. 2).

[20] In the following I shall eschew detailed references, since, on the whole, I rely on standard accounts as well as on the material in the following two Parts and in other of my works, all of which are cited in the "Bibliography". Two older general accounts of this period still very much worth consulting are Kurt Reindel's, "Die politische Entwicklung", and Friedrich Prinz', "Die innere Entwicklung", both in the second edition of the *Handbuch der bayerischen Geschichte*, which now is supplemented by the *Handbuch der bayerischen Kirchengeschichte*. For monolinguals, there is Herwig Wolfram's excellent, "Bavaria in the tenth and early eleventh centuries", in the third volume of *The New Cambridge Medieval History*, which also has Eckhard Müller-Mertens complementary, "The Ottonians as Kings and Emperors". For the earlier period see also Johannes Fried's "The Frankish Kingdoms, 817-911: The East and Middle Kingdoms", in the preceding Cambridge volume. The general course of German history in this period is covered in Timothy Reuter's uniquely valuable though (now) older, *Germany in the early middle ages, c. 800-1056*.

[21] C. Hammer, "The handmaid's tale: morganatic relationships in early-medieval Bavaria", esp. pp. 359-60; T. Kohl, *Lokale Gesellschaften. Formen der Gemeinschaft in Bayern vom 8. Bis zum 10. Jahrhundert*, pp. 195-200.

relatives, and they controlled substantial economic resources which they were able to dispose at times according to their wishes. Thus, they often can be important for understanding political developments. This was certainly true of Duke Tassilo's "duchess", Liutpirc, to the extent that she was personally vilified by Charlemagne's propagandists.[22] We have good reason to suspect that the consorts of the mighty Ebersberger comital dynasty discussed here in Part Two (II.7) were often remarkable persons in their own right. But women were, nonetheless, excluded from direct participation in the early-medieval political community as were the ministerials.

Interestingly, this restriction also applies to a group of free men, the clergy, who lived in a kind of alternative political community, subject to different laws and structures of authority than laymen. Like women and the unfree, they had to proceed in legal actions and disputes through a lay steward or proxy (*advocatus*). However, this clerical community was, at the same time, an integral part of any early-medieval "state" because its sacral powers, its economic resources, its genealogical connections, its administrative expertise, and its learning were indispensible to political, economic and social life. Under the Ottonian rulers of the tenth century one logical variant of this situation was pursued, and the Crown's co-option of the ideology, resources and apparatus of the church became extraordinarily thoroughgoing. At all times, lay rulers and leading clerics were both extremely attentive to each others' interests to the point where any notion of separation of powers is illusory. The great councils which rulers convened from time to time usually included both secular and church magnates although we are better informed about ecclesiastical agendas, since they became part of the church's institutional memory in the canon law. The clergy, particularly the higher clergy, bishops and abbots, certainly participated in the political community but were not entirely of it.

Finally, there were marginal groups. Perhaps surprisingly, ethnicity of itself did not determine participation, since persons of – apparently – Slavic and Roman origins were included on the same basis as ethnic Bavarians: that is, on the basis of residence, free status and property. However, Jews, as we shall see in Part I.3, were not included even though they might engage freely in wide ranging commercial activities, amass considerable property, and occupy a significant position in their local community. Like unfree royal servants, they were directly dependent on the Crown.

In sum, the political community of Bavaria throughout our period consisted of free men who were also (so far as we can tell) landed proprietors. This is not so odd. It was, after all, the basis of the European political model into the 19th and even the 20th century. Nevertheless, this limited though not inconsiderable political community of the legally free still encompassed a very large social and economic spectrum from great imperial aristocrats to modest country squires barely distinguishable from prosperous dependent peasants.[23] In Bavaria, aside from the aristocratic dynasties or *genealogiae* of the ducal family, the Agilolfings, and of the five somewhat elusive other lineages who were accorded (solely) higher wergelds or monetary compensations than ordinary freemen, there was no legally-established nobility. In early-medieval Bavarian records the terms "liber" and "nobilis" are often used interchangeably. These are the numerous persons we meet in the abundant records of property transactions and court suits preserved in the cartularies from this period: as donors, plaintiffs, defendants, witnesses, jurors and bystanders. Not all, of course, were equal members of the political community.

The political history of Bavaria during the 9th and 10th centuries is unfamiliar to most and inherently confusing, since not only did the rulers change, but the very type of rule itself fluctuated widely. In the eighth century the duchy was largely independent of the Frankish kingdom and ruled by its own ducal dynasty, the Agilolfings, whose last member was Tassilo. After that there was a period of uncertainty. It appears that in the early 790s Charlemagne's oldest son by his first wife, Pippin (known to us as the "Hunchback"), attempted to assume a kingship there like the ones that his younger half-brothers, Pippin and Ludwig, already held in Italy and the Aquitaine. This, however, was a short episode which

---

[22] C. Hammer, *From Ducatus to Regnum*, p. 192.
[23] See most recently the remarks in T. Kohl, *Lokale Gesellschaften. Formen der Gemeinschaft in Bayern vom 8. Bis zum 10. Jahrhundert*, p. 42, and his interesting discussion of deed witnesses, pp. 318-22. The much older work by Franz Gutmann, *Die Soziale Gliederung der Bayern zur Zeit des Volksrechtes*, is still worth consulting, here: pp. 231-59.

ended badly in 792.[24] After Pippin's banishment to the monastery of Prüm, Charlemagne revived a governmental model used earlier in the century in Alemannia. As we shall see in Part Two, Bavaria was then subjected to powerful comital proconsuls, one in Old Bavaria (Gerold, ?-799; Audulf, 799-818) and another on the eastern frontier. Charlemagne's sole heir, Ludwig (known to us as the "Pious"), however, immediately revived the concept of a Bavarian kingship when he designated his oldest son, Lothar, as king there already in 814. This seems to have had little practical effect, nor were the earlier years of the reign of Lothar's younger brother, Ludwig (known to us as the "German") from 817 much different. The Bavarian proconsuls and their *comites* continued to rule Bavaria on behalf of its absent or disinterested Frankish "kings" who evidently regarded the country as a sort of royal appanage.

That changed fundamentally in 826 when young Ludwig himself came to Bavaria and particularly from 828 onwards when he returned with his wife, Hemma, the sister of the new imperial consort, Judith. Ludwig quickly established himself firmly as a royal ruler in Old Bavaria and began to expand his lordship in the East which soon became the principal base of his power. From there, during the troubled final years of his father who died in 840, he expanded his realm to include all of what was called "Eastern Francia" in the dating clauses of his charters, and this wider realm was recognized by his brothers in the Treaty of Verdun in 843. Under Ludwig, Bavaria continued to be a core territory of "Eastern Francia", but after his death in 876 and the division of his realm, it passed separately to his oldest son, Karlmann (r. 876-880), who may have designated himself as "king of the Bavarians" and certainly as "king of Bavaria". Even though Karlmann's son and ultimate heir, Arnolf (r. 887-899), did not use an ethnic title, he clearly based his expanded rule over Francia and then the Empire on Bavaria with, as we shall see in Part One (I.2), his principal seat in Regensburg. With Arnolf's young son, Ludwig (r. 900-911, and known to us as the "Child"), the last of the East Frankish Carolingians, the locus of kingship then passed from Bavaria first to Francia and shortly thereafter to Saxony.

Throughout the long 9th century under the Carolingians, Bavaria occupied a central position in the East Frankish polity and was under some form of direct royal rule. In practice, however, these later Carolingian kings like Charlemagne and Ludwig the Pious continued to rely on powerful proconsuls in Old Bavaria: Ernst (?-861), Engildeo (?-895), and Luitpold (895-907), the first two of whom evidently asserted themselves too vigorously and were deposed. The last of these proconsuls, Luitpold, probably a relative of the last two Carolingians, led the Bavarian army into a disastrous defeat against the Magyars where he was killed along with numerous magnates and churchmen. His son, Arnulf (r. 907/11-937), may have felt himself to have a legitimate claim on the royal title in succession to his kinsman, King Ludwig the Child. But, in the event, he was passed over, and, instead, he re-established a strong and independent ducal polity in Bavaria, initially in opposition to his Frankish rival, King Konrad I (r. 911-918), and to the first Saxon Ottonian ruler, King Heinrich I (r. 919-936). It appears that the Carolingian Karlmann's brief rule as King of the Bavarians was Arnulf's model. Duke Arnulf was succeeded by his son, Eberhard, who, however, quickly ran afoul of the powerful new Ottonian ruler, Otto I (r. 936-973, and known to us as the "Great"), but Arnulf's brother, Berthold then quickly was admitted as duke (r. 938-947). Thereafter, all the dukes of Bavaria were junior (and often disgruntled) members of the Ottonian family, the first of whom, Heinrich I (r. 948-955), was married to Duke Arnulf's daughter, Judith, from whom two other dukes were descended. The only agnatic exception from the short-lived Luitpolding dynasty was Duke Heinrich III (r. 983-985), the son of Duke Berthold, who was also the first duke of the new duchy of Carinthia.

Thus, rule in Bavaria fluctuated from an ethnic duchy under an indigenous duke and hereditary dynasty (-788), to, possibly, a short-lived kingdom, to a Frankish prefecture (788-817), to a Carolingian kingdom of varying autonomy and visibility within Eastern Francia (817-911), back to an ethnic duchy under an indigenous duke and his dynasty (907-947), and finally to Ottonian house duchy from 947. The ethnic self-identities of the later rulers are largely unknown to us. Only Duke Tassilo, King Ludwig the German in his early years, King Karlmann and Duke Arnulf apparently used Bavarian identifiers of their rule in their official documents. It is very important to note, however, that throughout these wide political fluctuations, the territorial integrity of Bavaria was maintained essentially "as Tassilo held it".

---

[24] C. Hammer, "*Pipinus Rex*: Pippin's Plot of 792 and Bavaria".

Evidently, the country had acquired a certain historical legitimacy independent of its ruler which was not easily altered until the very late 10th century with the creation of a separate Carinthian duchy which, significantly, was initially entrusted to a Bavarian Luitpolding. During our two centuries Bavaria always had a single ruler ruling over a stable geographical entity.

There is little evidence, however, that these rulers were particularly active in administration. The dukes, with the assistance of friendly clergy, had only some very limited capacity to formulate and promulgate written instruments. The Frankish rulers did have royal and imperial chanceries, but there is no indication that their attention was specially directed to Bavarian administration or even particularly to Bavarian matters. Thus, it is quite clear that a professional bureaucracy, an institution which plays a major role in Professor Strayer's "state", played no significant role in establishing and maintaining any early-medieval Bavarian state. Likewise, taxes do not seem to have been levied. Aside from legal fines, tolls, excises and occasional "gifts" (Part I.3), kings and dukes were still expected to live from the proceeds of their fiscal estates. Thus, to use Chris Wickham's terminology, Bavaria was clearly a "land/rent-based state", rather than a "tax-based state".[25] As he points out, this fact places serious limitations on the ruler, since land is finite and property grants can lead to regional fragmentation. At one point the ducal fisc, appropriated by the Carolingians, must have been quite extensive and probably included some ancient Roman fiscal properties. The annexation of Carinthia after 772 must have added significantly to it. But, in our period, we only know the extent of the fisc 'negatively' from the numerous alienated properties referred to in various deeds.[26]

As elsewhere in the early Middle Ages, secular administration in Bavaria seems to have been largely oral and *ad hoc* although, within those limitations, it could still be quite effective. A prime reason for suspecting effective, albeit limited government throughout these two centuries is the strong element of administrative continuity provided by the comital organization established under Charlemagne which we shall examine in Part Two. However, one fundamental change relevant to our immediate concerns does seem to have occurred. Early in the 9th century we have records of several large comital assemblies in Old Bavaria resulting from missatical visits and the promulgation of capitulary legislation by the Frankish rulers. These were not deliberative or even representative assemblies. They were, in the first instance, instruments of imperial communication and control. Still, by their very existence they must have promoted a sense of common identity and purpose amongst their participants. We do not know whether similar assemblies occurred in the Bavarian East, but we do know that in western Old Bavaria they evidently ceased under Ludwig the German and were revived thereafter only on a very occasional basis. Thus, a prime means for bringing together the obvious leaders of the Bavarian political community and of building solidarity amongst them was discarded. After this the royal or ducal court must have been the primary forum for assembling the Bavarian magnates for a common enterprise, but now selectivity and royal favoritism could play a much larger role.

The primary regular assemblies of Bavarians throughout our period were, rather, the local comital courts which – presumably – were held throughout the country. There, so it will be argued in Part Two, the *comites* who served as conveners and judges – whatever their personal prerogatives and (often considerable) resources – remained royal or ducal officials serving at the pleasure of the ruler. The Bavarian Law Code, in a section probably drafted under Charlemagne, specifies that these courts should be held fortnightly by the relevant *comes* with a *iudex* or judge present, and a law book should be available "so that they may always render a right judgment" (Exhibit II.1).[27] Although the Code was first drafted in the mid-8th century under the Agilolfing dukes and contains even older material, it was still being copied in Bavaria into the 12th century and beyond.[28] And in the early 11th century we have a surprising and vivid witness to a powerful Bavarian count's concern with the written Bavarian law and its study (Part II.8). Early-medieval law was, of course, personal law as versions of the Code circulating

---

[25] C. Wickham, *Framing the Early Middle Ages*, pp. 58-59.
[26] Friedrich Prinz's 1962 article on this issue, "Herzog und Adel im agilulfingischen Bayern", has still not been supplanted.
[27] *Lex Bav.*, p. 308: *semper rectum iudicium iudicent*.
[28] R. Kottje, "Die Lex Baiuvariorum – Das Recht der Baiern", analyzes the manuscript tradition, here the Table on p. 20. Comment on use also in C. Hammer, "*Lex scripta* in early medieval Bavaria".

outside Bavaria demonstrate, but it could also have a territorial function where all members of the political community were subject to it. The Bavarian Law Code was the only written instrument of secular government which maintained its validity everywhere in Bavaria throughout our period, and I strongly suspect that a common law was a powerful instrument for creating a common polity.

Although the early-medieval church stood to some degree apart from the secular political order, nevertheless, it remained an essential component of early-medieval governance. It also must have played a fundamental role in shaping the Bavarian polity. Under Tassilo, Bavaria was not a separate metropolitan diocese, but neither were Bavarian bishops suffragans of the archbishopic of Mainz which comprised the other eastern Frankish dioceses including those of neighboring Augsburg and Eichstätt. This lack of an archbishop – who, in fact, seems to have been included in the papacy's original plan for Bavaria – evidently resulted from deliberate and consistent efforts by the earliest Bavarian dukes who wished to avoid any Frankish entanglements by establishing direct ecclesiastical relations with the papacy. This singular policy began with Duke Theodo's unprecedented "pilgrimage" to Rome in 716 as the "first of that people". Moreover, under Duke Tassilo in the 770s at the ducal estate of Dingolfing all six Bavarian bishops and 13 abbots from the most important Bavarian monasteries formally associated themselves for common memorial observances which was an obvious reflex of a similar association established by Frankish bishops at Attigny in 762. This Bavarian spiritual association was, thus, clearly political in its intent to maintain a separate identity for the church in Bavaria, and it was successful enough to serve as a model for a similar association under Duke Arnulf in 932 to which Eichstätt was now joined as a Bavarian diocese.

Perhaps surprisingly, this Bavarian ecclesiastical separatism was decisively strengthened in 798 after the Carolingian "Anschluss" when Salzburg was elevated to metropolitan rank over the other Bavarian dioceses. This dignity and the fact that it was Salzburg, not Regensburg, which now headed the archdiocese was probably a result of Charlemagne's high regard for its bishop, Arn. But one wonders whether the creation of a formal Bavarian archdiocese was also part of a larger plan to create a Bavarian kingdom which, as we have just seen, was clearly in some minds at this time. All Bavarian rulers relied on their bishops' loyalty to maintain their rule. In the early years of Duke Arnulf's reign the Bavarian church sided with King Heinrich I against him. Obtaining their submission became the primary item in Arnulf's negotiations with Heinrich in 922 when the duke's authority to designate Bavarian bishops was recognized by Heinrich, and the bishops acknowledged Arnulf as their duke. Arnulf's ducal powers over the Bavarian church may have been exceptional in their virtually "royal" extent, but throughout our period the Bavarian political and ecclesiastical orders were coterminous and generally co-operative. Such a long-lasting coincidence of the two supreme authorities, spiritual and temporal, must have been primary source of a common Bavarian identity. Unfortunately, evidence for provincial synods where all Bavarian dioceses would have been present is scanty. It does not appear that Salzburg exercised strong or particularly active authority over its suffragans.

Military matters were a major preoccupation of all early-medieval rulers and a major burden on resources. Ability to raise a common army was an essential characteristic of any respectable state. According to the Bavarian Law Code (Title 2.5), the army was to be led by the duke but evidently raised by the *comites* within their jurisdictions who then led their contingents in the field. But this provision for raising the shire levy of freemen and composed largely of foot soldiers became increasingly anachronistic during our period as highly-trained and armed mounted retainers of the ruler, of lay magnates and of the principal churches became increasingly important agents in warfare. This shift from part-time to professional warriors may have diminished opportunities for broad regional and inter-regional co-operation and, thus, for a common identity. But it was a military necessity and would have facilitated occasional major expeditions outside the country – with mixed success. Apparently under the old military regime, Duke Tassilo annexed Carinthia in 772, the last major expansion of Bavarian territory; under the new military regime, Duke Arnulf's father, Luitpold, was able to mobilize and lead a large Bavarian force including high churchmen down the Danube to disaster at Pressburg/Bratislava in 907. Still, military successes could be important politically. Effective protection against foreign enemies has always been a primary source of subjects' loyalties. Much of Duke Arnulf's resilient legitimacy in Bavaria must have derived from his early successes against Magyar raiders just as Otto the Great is still chiefly celebrated for his great victory over them at the river Lech in 955. But one has the general impression that decentralized frontier raiding in the East dominated Bavarian martial activities.

Less bellicose commercial matters also promoted Bavarian unity. In Part One (I.3) we shall examine the network of tolls and regional markets which were evidently based on fiscal estates and controlled by comital officials. Within this network, Bavarians of whatever ethnicity enjoyed certain exemptions not extended to foreigners trading or sojourning there which implies a certain sense of national citizenship. Bavaria also developed a distinctive coinage as the Frankish mint established at Regensburg under Ludwig the German became increasingly important during the 9th century, and its die was used in the other Bavarian mints created at Eichstätt, Neuburg, Freising, Passau and Salzburg during the course of the 10th and 11th centuries (Part I.2).

It is impossible to determine precisely how important any of these various factors were in the construction of Bavarian "stateliness". What we can say, however, is that early-medieval Bavaria was no mere collection of a random permanent population living within relatively stable borders. There was clearly a certain internal coherence which was maintained over a very long period indeed. I doubt that this polity was a "strong state" as has been argued recently and vigorously for contemporary late Anglo-Saxon England.[29] The precocious bureaucratic development evident there which made extensive use of written instruments is quite absent from Bavaria as is a regular system of taxation. But Bavaria's coherence seems to meet and even exceed the minimal requirements of a "state". I think it could fairly be designated as a "weak state" in Chris Wickham's scheme, "with a landed army but also a strong sense of public power acting as a focus for political legitimation".[30] Was it also a "sovereign state" as the fourth element in the Montevideo Convention seems to require? Clearly, at various points it met this common test of sovereignty: independence in international relations. Duke Tassilo certainly conducted himself as a sovereign ruler in this sense, as did, less controversially, King Karlmann – who even added an Italian reign to his Bavarian – and so also did Duke Arnulf for large portions of his reign. And throughout our period Bavarian rulers exercised, in practice, exclusive authority within the country with the (important) exceptions of purely clerical and seigneurial jurisdiction and subject to occasional interventions by the Crown.[31]

Does this discussion then validate the Bavarian government's surprising claim that Bavaria is one of the oldest European states? Within certain limits it does. By the later 8th century something which could reasonably be called a "Bavarian state" certainly existed although its territorial extent reached far beyond the modern German "Land" while, on the other hand, not including all of it. The real reservation here regards the continuity of this undoubted early-medieval state into the modern period. In the late 10th century the great issue for the future of the Bavarian state was the final eclipse of the old Frankish model of strong, unitary royal governance and the multiplication, rather, of numerous important lay lordships and ecclesiastical immunities within its territory which we associate with the feudal regime of the high Middle Ages. The new feudal Bavaria can be seen clearly in the excellent map of "Bavaria around 1200" in the *Historical Atlas of Bavaria*.[32] Our discussion ends on the very eve of this fundamental development, and we will not consider here whether this momentous change compromised Bavarian "stateliness" although it certainly must have transformed its character. In the following two essays, we shall address only the earliest beginnings of this new feudal order in the 10th century with the first grants of regalian privileges to several bishoprics (Part I.2) and with the origins and development of the extensive lordship of the Ebersberger counts (Part II.4-8) which, so it will be argued, can serve as a model for the establishment of numerous other feudal dynasties which proliferated within Bavaria. We will leave Bavaria with its claim as "one of the oldest states in Europe" still intact.

---

[29] See the remarks in P. Wormald, "Pre-modern 'state' and 'nation'", pp. 181-85; and the essays by James Campbell collected in his *The Anglo-Saxon State*.
[30] C. Wickham, *Framing the Early Middle Ages*, p. 56, although I think that any Bavarian concepts of "public power" were inherited through the Franks rather than directly from the Romans.
[31] This is similar to what political scientists designate as "Westphalian sovereignty". See Michael Goodhart's review article discussing current approaches to this concept by political scientists: "Sovereignty: Reckoning What is Real", here: pp. 243-44.
[32] *Bayerischer Geschichtsatlas*, Map. 18/19 a/b, with commentary by Gertrud Diepolder on pp. 76-77.

Part I. Borough and Marketplace

Proto- and Para-Urbanism in Early-Medieval Bavaria

I.1 Early-Medieval Bavaria, an Urban Backwater?

Bavaria is not noted as an exceptional medieval urban landscape. In Franconia to the northwest and Swabia to the west one finds many of the sleepy and romantic small towns and imperial cities that one associates with Germany.[1] But within the central regions of Old Bavaria such little "urban republics" are absent, and, with a few notable exceptions such as Landshut, a former ducal residence, the country towns and provincial markets are quite modest places. The one major city that most people associate with Bavaria, Munich, did not – as we shall see – exist before the mid-twelfth century. The lone Bavarian medieval metropolis, Regensburg on the Danube, is largely unknown to foreigners although, unlike its medieval counterparts Cologne, Mainz and Munich, it escaped devastation during the Second World War and has preserved its extensive and remarkable medieval core intact.

This lack of "urbanity" was, to some extent, prefigured under the Romans. Early-medieval Bavaria occupied three late-Roman provinces: *Raetia II* in the diocese of Italy and *Noricum Ripense* and *Noricum Mediterraneanum* in the diocese of Illyria.[2] These provinces, *Raetia* and *Noricum*, in separate dioceses and customs' districts divided by the River Inn, contained two quite distinct urban cultures.[3] *Noricum*, which had been an independent kingdom, had a vibrant economy, local culture and several major cities. In the northern portion, *Noricum Ripense*, which stretched along the south bank of the Danube, there were at least four *municipia*: the provincial capital, *Ovilava* (Wels); *Lauriacum* (Lorch), which was the site of the legionary fortress and the only attested bishopric; *Cetium* (St Pölten); and *Iuvavum* (Salzburg).[4] In contrast, *Raetia* had only two cities of note: the first provincial capital at *Cambodunum* (Kempten) and its successor, *Augusta Vindelicum* (Augsburg), both of which lay west of the River Lech and, thus, in Alemannia and largely outside the political boundaries of early-medieval Bavaria.[5]

We learn something about the tenuous urban existence in the Raetian border *oppidum* of *Batavis* (Passau) from Eugippius' incomparable "Account" of St Severin with its vivid description of the garrison's destruction and the saint's attempted evacuation of the place.[6] Indeed, *Raetia II* east of the River Lech appears to have been a heavily-militarized frontier province largely geared to supporting its resident legion. The province's most impressive surviving relic is the legionary fortress at *Castra Regina* (Regensburg) on the Danube with its Praetorian Gate (still) facing enemy territory across the great

---

[1] There are concise histories of many Bavarian towns with bibliographies in the new edition of the *Handbuch der Historischen Stätten, Bayern I*. Voluminous historical and statistical evidence for all urban places within the modern *Land* of Bavaria is also collected systematically in the topographical entries of the *Bayerisches Städtebuch*, with an overview of urban development in Bavaria by G. Pfeiffer in Part 2, pp. 25-31, here. p. 26: "Das Ergebnis [of fragmented authority in Franconia and Swabia] ist im Vergleich zum Herzogtum Bayern eine viel stärkere Dichte von Märkten und Städten im fränkisch-schwäbischen Bereich ..." For Franconia, see, for example, the treasures exhibited in *Reichsstädte in Franken*.

[2] Bavaria conquered the territory of the adjacent Norican province south of the Alps, *Noricum Mediterraneanum*, in 772 which subsequently became the separate duchy of Carinthia in 976 (Introduction). Even though it played a significant role in Bavarian political history, this heavily urbanized province, which bordered on Italian Venetia, is not considered in this paper, since its ancient and important urban centers – to the extent which they survived the Slavic invasions – were not significant for early-medieval Bavaria (in addition to G. Alföldy, *Noricum*, pp. 96-103, see also the archaeological gazetteer in F. Glaser, *Frühes Christentum im Alpenraum*, pp. 94-147).

[3] For the cultural differences see: S. von Schnurbein, "Die Kulturgeschichtliche Stellung des nördlichen Rätiens"; for the provincial border along the Inn see: G. Ulbert, "Zur Grenze zwischen den römischen Provinzen Norikum und Raetien am Inn".

[4] G. Alföldy, *Noricum*, pp. 96-103.

[5] W. Czysz, "Das zivile Leben in der Provinz", pp. 198-212, with accompanying "Gazetteer" entries. Augsburg is evidently the "splendidissima Raetiae provinciae colonia", mentioned by Tacitus, where, unusually, the the loyal Hermunduri were allowed to trade (*Germania* 41/1).

[6] *Vita Severini*, cc. 19-22; see the archaeological reviews of Severin's places by H. Ubl, "Die archäologische Erforschung der Severinsorte", and R. Christlein, Die rätischen Städte Severins"; for the text see most recently C. Hammer, "'The Examples of the Saints".

river. Regensburg, of course, also had a significant civilian settlement, the *canabae legionis*, serving the garrison, but there is no evidence for any advanced urban organization.[7]

After the establishment of Frankish ducal rule sometime in the mid-sixth century, Augsburg, the former provincial capital, may have served initially as the principal center of ducal authority, but during the seventh century it appears to have been supplanted by Regensburg because of the intact fortification there and better location.[8] Nevertheless, the early dukes also exercised their authority from numerous fiscal estates scattered throughout the countryside, and it would be anachronistic to speak of a "capital". To the East in *Noricum*, the border zone against the nomadic Avars (and later, the Magyars) began at the River Enns, the site of *Lauriacum*, so that the Roman cities in *Noricum*, with the exception of Salzburg, were (as we shall see in Part I.3) largely marginalized as frontier outposts within a militarized, marcher organization. Thus, although Roman populations speaking the Latin language and even preserving some artifacts of Roman organization and culture survived around certain places such as Passau, Salzburg, and Augsburg, it is mistaken to speak of urban continuity – as opposed to continuity of place – in early-medieval Bavaria.[9] Edith Ennen was certainly right when in 1956 she wrote that in contrast to the Rhineland, "along the Danube there was an almost total collapse of urban life".[10] In Bavaria there was no "Transformation of the Roman World"; with a few notable exceptions noted below, it simply vanished and a largely new beginning was made.

I.2 Proto-Urbanism and Boroughs

Nevertheless, it is in these old Roman centers that we must look for the first signs of "proto-urbanism" in Bavaria. Here I employ a term, a translation of the German word "Frühurbanismus", which now is well established in the English-language literature.[11] By this I mean a form of urbanism which differs – in some respects, significantly – from the archetypical autonomous mercantile community of the high and later Middle Ages but which still possesses certain distinctive characteristics which differentiate it sharply from the early-medieval economic and social organization of the agrarian countryside. Proto-urbanism can be specified more precisely using a "bundle" of criteria or indicators of urbanity.[12] I have selected eleven criteria which conform to those identified in other studies of early-medieval urbanism, are relevant to Bavaria, and can, in some way, be documented from the extant sources, both historical and archaeological. I have then arrayed these criteria against six places (see Sketch-Map).[13] Both axes of the resulting Exhibit I.1 require some explanation.

---

[7] For the *cannabae* at Regensburg see now: F. Loré, "Wohnraum statt Gräber – Cannabae legionis in Regensburg größer als erwartet".

[8] W. Störmer, "Augsburg zwischen Antike und Mittelalter", pp. 71, 76, citing a 2002 article by Arno Rettner which I have not been able to consult. For the difficulties in locating late 6th and early 7th century "Bavaria" see C. Hammer, "Early Merovingian Bavaria: A Late-Antique Italian Perspective", *Journal of Late Antiquity* (2011, forthcoming).

[9] For references to cultural continuity at Passau, see C. Hammer, "For All the Saints", pp. 11-12 ; the notable medieval pilgrimage to the shrine of St Afra, just south of the Roman walls of Augsburg, is attested well into the sixth century by Venantius Fortunatus. The area within the Roman city walls was certainly inhabited in the early medieval period; the remains of a wooden weaving shed, evidence of a substantial establishment, have been excavated in the area near the cathedral (V. Babucke, "Die Ausgrabungen 'Hinter dem Schwalbeneck 5-9' in Augsburg".

[10] English translation: E. Ennen, "Different Types of Formation of European Towns", p. 175; so also W. Schlesinger, "Der Markt als Frühform der deutschen Stadt", p. 270: "Generell wird man sagen dürfen, daß an der Donau die Kontinuität aus der Spätantike weniger startk ausgeprägt war als am Rhein." In my view, their qualifications are unnecessary.

[11] So in several of the contributions for the earliest period in *The Cambridge Urban History of Britain*, e.g. pp. 30, 35, 79 and 127.

[12] There is a discussion of these criteria in R. Hodges, *Dark Age Economics*, pp. 20-25; and in C. Wickham, *Framing the Early Middle Ages*, pp. 592-93, favoring economic criteria; Wickham's book contains a very good general survey of "Cities" (pp. 591-692) and "Systems of Exchange", pp. 693-824. For an "applied" use of this concept, see especially the very thoughtful list in *The Erosion of History; Archaeology and Planning in Towns*, pp. 8-9. H. Dopsch applies six criteria to Salzburg in *Geschichte Salzburgs*, pp. 677-79. I am puzzled by David Palliser's evident endorsement in his "Introduction" to *The Cambridge Urban History* (p. 5), of Susan Reynolds's blanket rejection of this useful concept ("The Writing of medieval urban history in England", pp. 49-50).

[13] There are topographical entries *sub nomine* in the *Bayerisches Städtebuch* for Eichstätt in Part 1 (Franconia) and for Augsburg, Freising, Passau and Regensburg in Part 2 (Swabia and Bavaria).

Although four of the six places had significant "Roman Predecessors", this does not, of itself, signify urban continuity. Rather, it merely shows that the Romans were adept at picking sites for their towns which then prospered because of their advantageous locations just as towns did in the medieval period and still do in the modern world. Moreover, Roman antecedents could be important for early-medieval towns, since there may have been a legacy of infrastructure, physical or administrative, which could be reused. These four places have been introduced already: Regensburg, Passau, Salzburg and Augsburg. We shall see that at Regensburg the remaining legionary fortifications were clearly a significant determinant of its future development. The sites of the other two places, Eichstätt and Freising, were both within the Roman *limes* (Eichstätt until the mid-3rd century when the border was retracted to the Rhine and Danube), but neither has yielded evidence of significant urban settlement. Two places were outside Bavaria proper. By the later eighth century Augsburg lay in Alemannia, but its diocese extended into western Bavaria, and its influence there seems to have been considerable.[14] Eichstätt began as an Anglo-Saxon foundation with strong Bavarian connections but, like Augsburg, it belonged to the archdiocese of Mainz and pertained, in its early years, to the Frankish, not Bavarian political sphere. However, in the course of the 9th and 10th centuries Eichstätt was increasingly integrated into the Bavarian polity. It would be difficult to find any other likely candidates for "proto-urbanism" in early-medieval Bavaria.[15]

The criterion of "Transportation Access" shows that five of them were located on the Roman road system and all on navigable rivers – Eichstätt along the Frankish "Nibelungen Road" between Worms and Regensburg. Of course, not all access was equally good. The Rivers Lech and Isar were marginal for boats, especially in dry seasons, and the road by Freising was clearly secondary. Augsburg, at the head of the *Via Claudia*, the great Roman highway south over the Alps directly to Verona by the Fern and Reschen Passes was particularly well located. Regensburg, too, had good routes to Italy by highway connections over the Brenner Pass, the ancient *Via Vipitena*. Regensburg, Passau, and, less directly, Salzburg all had ready access to the eastern Bavarian frontier along the Danube River, the great central European East-West transportation corridor into modern times.

The survival of parts of the Roman road system into the early Middle Ages is an important evidence for continuity of infrastructure. The other is "Fortification". When Bishop of Arbeo of Freising described Regensburg around 770 in his "Life" of St Emmeram, the first thing he noted was, "a borough (*urbs*) built of hewn stones ... a capital (*metropolim*), a citadel (*arce*) for this people ... an impregnable borough (*urbs inexpugnabilis*) of squared stones with high towers", before going on to note the abundance of wells (*puteis habundans*)![16] Both the still-visible fortifications and, presumably, the wells were a highly-valued Roman inheritance which was put to early use by the dukes who located their court complex within the eastern part of the legionary fortress (City Plan).[17] This marked their court at Regensburg off sharply from their numerous rural residences which were, like those of the Frankish kings, unfortified.

Indeed, I was surprised at the centrality of fortifications in early references to Bavarian towns. The towns located at the outflow of the River Regen on the Danube and on the River Salzach were "-burgs" or boroughs: Regens-burg and Salz-burg, respectively, with no need for further descriptive qualifiers in the earliest deeds and charters. In both cases (certainly for *Iuvavum*/Salzburg), their fortified character had trumped their Roman names.[18] Likewise, Augsburg apparently did not become a "-burg" until Bishop Ulrich rebuilt its dilapidated fortifications in the mid-10th century. Freising was not a Roman town, but the fortifications on the cathedral hill dominated its earliest designations; it was a "castrum" and a "castellum".[19] The late-Roman "oppidum" of *Batavis* was fortified, and the fortified character of

---

[14] For the early ecclesiastical histories of Augsburg and Eichstätt, as well as for the other bishoprics, see now the relevant sections of the *Handbuch der bayerischen Kirchengeschichte*.

[15] I here exclude the episcopal seat at Säben, then Brixen, on the south side of the Alps, which, although it was part of the Bavarian Church, had a distinctive history because of its location and was probably not part of Bavaria until the mid-8th century.

[16] Here and elsewhere when I translate "urbs" as "borough" I do so to emphasize its fortified character as in the Anglo-Saxon "bur(g)h" or German "burg" (see below), not to imply that it had some chartered status as characterized later medieval English boroughs; see the discussion of "borough" in S. Reynolds, "The Writing of medieval urban history in England", pp. 47-48.

[17] See the excellent archaeological survey in A. Boos *et al.*, "Regensburg zwischen Antike und Mittelalter", pp. 35-36.

[18] For the complex history of the name "Regensburg" see K. Dietz and T. Fischer, *Die Römer in Regensburg*, pp. 26-28.

[19] See the references assembled in R. Brandl-Ziegert, "Die Sozialstruktur der bayerischen Bischofs- und Residenzstädte Passau,

the episcopal seat at Passau continued to be emphasized, albeit not so exclusively as at Freising.[20] In 908 the bishop of Eichstätt received a valuable royal charter to establish a market and mint and collect market tolls.[21] The proceeds were to be used to put up defenses against the Magyars.[22] In the wording of the charter, "to establish a borough (*urbem construere*)" was the same as "to erect fortifications (*munitiones ... moliri*)". In the 8th, 9th and 10th centuries before the proliferation of feudal castles across the countryside which we shall explore in Part II, the distinctive fortifications of these few towns were clearly recognized by contemporaries as a sure indication of their urbanity.[23]

The site of a "Ducal or Royal Palace", an " Early Episcopal Seat" or a "Major Monastery" could, but need not, make a settlement important as a central administrative place and the locus of industry and trade. All six places were the seats of 8th-century bishoprics, and we tend to equate the Latin word "civitas" or "city" with an episcopal city.[24] But early-medieval Bavarian scribes were more circumspect. "Civitas" was, indeed, used to designate an episcopal city or, at least, the bishop's portion of the city as at Passau; Augsburg, in one of the earliest references to it, is "civitas Augusta".[25] However, in the abundant documents of the Freising cartulary the term is used rarely and then not for Freising but for Regensburg, Vicenza and Augsburg, perhaps in deference to their more venerable status?[26] It is very doubtful whether *Raetia II* had ever been organized by the Romans into a network of urban territories or "civitates", each centered on a principal town as in Italy and Gaul, which then were "transformed" directly into early-medieval bishoprics and comital jurisdictions.[27] Here in Bavaria there was simply no heritage to "transform" and the available Latin vocabulary had to be adapted to the actual circumstances.

Nevertheless, these six places were also important administrative centers of early-medieval Bavaria. The dukes preceded the Church by more than a century. In the early 8th century, before the Bonifacian (re-)organization of episcopal structures in 738/9, the dukes had courts at Regensburg, Passau, Salzburg and Freising, each of them, at one time, ruling over a territory that was subsequently converted into a diocese.[28] However, only the ducal court at Regensburg retained its prominence into the 9th and 10th centuries for reasons alluded to above. Augsburg was at the very eastern edge of Alemannia. The ducal dynasty of Alemannia, which was terminated in the 740s, was closely related to that of Bavaria; it is not known whether it maintained an establishment at Augsburg. In any event, Augsburg did not become prominent in royal and imperial politics until the early 11th century under the Salian dynasty.[29]

Regensburg, on the other hand, became the site of the Frankish royal court already under Charlemagne between 791 and 793, and it remained a principal royal seat for the East Frankish Carolingian dynasty during the 9th century, particularly under the King and Emperor Arnolf (r. 886/897-899) who apparently

---

Freising, Landshut und Ingolstadt", pp. 57-58.

[20] R. Brandl-Ziegert, "Die Sozialstruktur", p. 21; for the 8th-century evidence from Salzburg, see the exhaustive discussion of terms by Fritz Losek in his edition of, *Notitia Arnonis* und *Breves Notitiae*, pp. 65-70.

[21] MGH, Diplomata, Ludwig the Child, Nr 58, here: p. 186. See below.

[22] For comment see C. Bowlus, *The Battle of the Lechfeld and its Aftermath*, pp. 138-44.

[23] See the lexical discussion in G. Kobler, "*Civitas* und *vicus, burg, stat, dorf* und *wik*", p. 75: "für diese Burg nicht die kaufmännischen Bewohner, sondern die Mauer entscheidend ist". See also Michael Mitterauer's remarks cited in the Preface (fn. 1).

[24] In 798 Salzburg was elevated to metropolitan status over Regensburg, Passau, Freising and Säben. Augsburg and Eichstätt remained suffragans of the very large province of Mainz. Even before the formal creation of a separate archdiocese, the Church in Bavaria had – by the political design of the Bavarian dukes – been largely autonomous and independent of Mainz and, thus, of Frankish control.

[25] Citations in R. Brandl-Ziegert, "Die Sozialstruktur", p. 21; see next note for Augsburg and *Annales Regni Francorum, sub anno* 787 ("super civitatem Augustam").

[26] *Trad. Freising*, Nrs 197 ("civitatem qui vulgo nominator Reganespurc"), 400a ("in civitate Vincentia"), 475 ("ad episcopatum Auguste civitatis"), respectively. When it is used, uniquely, in connection with Freising, it seems to designate the diocese rather than the town itself; see Nr 415 (819): "venit ad sedem Frigisnensium civitatis".

[27] The Roman administrative territory of the provincial capital, Augsburg, may have survived into the early Middle Ages as the "Augstgau" (see W. Störmer, "Augsburg zwischen Antike und Mittelalter", p. 74); however, the urban organization of Noricum may have been more highly developed (G. Alföldy, *Noricum*, p. 102; *cf.* the early-medieval "Salzburggau").

[28] It is possible that some sort of royal establishment was maintained at Freising under King Ludwig the German, since we have evidence for a "comes palatinus" active there (C. Hammer, *From Ducatus to Regnum*, pp. 263-64).

[29] C. Brühl, "Augsburg" in his *Palatium und Civitas*, pp.193-218, here: 216-18.

built a royal palace to the southwest outside of the Roman fort and near to the important monastery of St Emmeram.[30] This extensive external area on the west side of the old legionary *castra* was then included in the major extension of the fortifications carried out under Duke Arnulf of Bavaria in the early 10th century (City Plan). The regular presence at Regensburg of imperial, royal and ducal courts and their periodic assemblies required other Bavarian magnates, bishops, abbots and counts, to establish their own urban "pied-a-terres" there, and within a century after Bishop Arbeo's effusive and premature encomium, we can begin to speak with confidence of Regensburg as a capital city.[31]

In many respects, the ecclesiastical structure was more centralized than the secular political structure. As we shall see in Part II, comital courts, the principal organs for secular administration, were normally held at various assembly places in the countryside including ducal and royal fiscal manors.[32] Synods and other ecclesiastical business might, likewise, be transacted at church estates outside the episcopal seats, and bishops did make their visitation rounds of their dioceses. But the surviving early cartularies from Freising, Regensburg and Passau and, from the 10th century from Salzburg, attest to a broadly-based lay piety that was centered on the cathedrals, and lay persons frequently had recourse to their diocesan seat to transact a variety of business with episcopal officials. Likewise, all of the early Bavarian bishoprics had monastic cathedral chapters and accommodated other monastic establishments within their towns. Some, most notably St Emmeram at Regensburg, became important spiritual and cultural centers at a European as well as a regional level, and the pilgrimage to the shrine of St Afra at Augsburg continued to be the most important in the northern Alpine piedmont. Thus, in many critical respects, administrative, economic and cultural, urban centrality at these six places was ensured primarily by the resident ecclesiastical institutions.

On the other hand, when we think of the medieval city, we think, in the first place of dynamic, secular, civic communities living by trade and industry with regular "Markets and Tolls", "Mints", and periodic "Fairs". However, there can be little doubt that the populations of these six places were composed largely of the seigneurial households of their resident lords: kings, dukes, bishops, abbots, counts and other dignitaries. In some places, almost certainly at Eichstätt and Freising and even at a place as important as Salzburg, these communities or *familiae* of dependents, most of whom were legally unfree, predominated.[33] If we look for evidences of free civic communities living by non-agricultural occupations, the search becomes much more difficult and indirect. Certainly, the presence of a market as an established place of exchange is one clue but, as we shall see in Part I.3, is not proof of a town, nor is it even indispensable.[34] The lords of these six places possessed extensive estates and claims to goods which were gathered and distributed through seigneurial command economies using their numerous dependents and officials. These might entail seigneurial "distribution centers" but not regular, public markets. Demand for rare and exotic goods could be met, as in the countryside, by itinerant traders and occasional fairs. It was not until these towns contained numerous and diverse populations living outside these seigneurial dependencies and their proprietary redistribution mechanisms that established, regular public markets became necessary. We might expect that this need first arose at Regensburg with its unique importance as an urban center of secular authority in addition to its major ecclesiastical establishments and its advantageous location for long-distance trade.

---

[30] See the comprehensive review in C. Brühl, "Regensburg", in his *Palatium und Civitas*, pp. 219-55, here: pp. 252-54; and now for the early-Carolingian palace W. Störmer, "Zur politische Bedeutung und zur topographischen Lage der Pfalz Karls des Großen in Regensburg". Nevertheless, A. Boos *et al.*, "Regensburg zwischen Antike und Mittelalter", pp. 37-39, note (p. 37) that, "die Diskussion über Lage und Aussehen der Pfalzen in Regensburg noch lange nicht beendet ist".

[31] For the increase in urban "courts" of ecclesiastical and lay magnates within the "castrum" near the ducal palace, see C. Brühl, "Regensburg" in his *Palatium und Civitas*, pp. 243-45.

[32] See below, Part II.1.

[33] So for Salzburg, H. Dopsch: "Die wichtigste Reservoir für die Entstehung und Ergänzung der Salzburger Bürgerschaft waren die Eigenleute des Erzbischofs, des Domkapitels und der Klöster" (*Geschichte Salzburgs*, p. 687). For the gradual and complex high-medieval transformation of urban seigneurial dependents into free citizens see K. Schulz, "Von der familia zur Stadtgemeinde", here for Regensburg: pp. 468-71; and B. Diestelkamp, "Freiheit der Bürger – Freiheit der Stadt".

[34] Thus, the thoughtful authors of *The Erosion of History* (p. 9) assert, in part anachronistically, that a market is, "Perhaps the only indispensable criterion [of a town], although a market alone does not distinguish a town."

The Carolingian and East Frankish kings (751-911/18) did not claim any exclusive, regalian right to establish markets which remained within the authority of local lords and the domain of ancient custom.[35] This royal prerogative was asserted aggressively, however, under the Saxon, Ottonian dynasty of the 10th century (919-1024). Indeed, the establishment of a market came then to be conjoined with the right to mint the coin to be used there and to collect the relevant tolls of those visiting the market which were both well established regalian rights. This triad, Market-Mint-Toll, first appears in the (surviving) East Frankish royal charters in 861 and was very rare thereafter until the 10th century.[36] The grant for Eichstätt in 908 referred to above was one of only five made for specific places under the East Frankish Carolingians. The other places in Bavaria to receive this privilege are almost a century later from the Emperor Otto III: Freising and Salzburg in 996 and Passau in 999, and, significantly, all of them were made, as at Eichstätt, to the respective bishops.[37]

The fact that all of these privileges are preserved in their original charters is an indication of their importance.[38] The need for regular and frequent access to markets is attested by the fact that those at Freising and Salzburg were to be held on a daily basis, the first instances of this provision in royal charters. The grant of minting privileges is, likewise, notable. Ninth-century Bavaria had only a single mint, established at Regensburg under King Ludwig II, known to us as "the German" (r. 817/26-876), but its early output was feeble.[39] Nevertheless, its location in the royal capital ensured its survival, and its die subsequently became the standard for coins struck by the other mints in Bavaria (and beyond): the "Regensburger Schlag". Trade can be carried on with limited minted specie, but a plentiful supply can only facilitate commerce and urbanism.[40] Finally, we know from a charter for the proprietary monastery at Donauwörth that Augsburg and Regensburg both held annual fairs by 1030 and probably much earlier.[41] It is notable, however, that we do not have similar "Market-Mint-Toll" charters for either Augsburg or Regensburg. At Augsburg this might be explained by the miserable survival of early documents, but not at Regensburg. Regensburg certainly had a market, since in the mid-10th century a Bavarian count made a grant to his monastery of a plot there "opposite the market" (*aream Ratispone iuxta mercatum sitam*).[42] It is more likely that a customary market had long existed there and that Regensburg's unique importance to the Crown prevented the delegation and resulting mediatization of important functions affecting economic life which were retained directly in the hands of royal agents.

It is at Regensburg that we have our first evidence for "Civic Organization" and "Civic Tenements" (Exhibit I.2).[43] It is, as we might expect, royal. In the early 880s a freeman, Ratheri, made a grant to the

---

[35] H. Adam, *Das Zollwesen im fränkischen Reich*, p. 186; the situation in West Francia, however, was more precocious in the 9th century and less prominent in the 10th century for which see the excellent survey in T. Endemann, *Markturkunde und Markt in Frankreich und Burgund*. There is a very useful survey from an urban history perspective with appended gazetteer of Carolingian, East Frankish and Ottonian royal charters of economic privileges by Friedrich Hardt-Friedrichs, "Markt, Münze und Zoll im ostfränkischen Reich".

[36] For the following, see the gazetteer in F. Hardt-Friedrichs, "Market, Münze und Zoll", pp. 21-31.

[37] MGH, Diplomata, Otto III, Nrs 197, 208 and 306. The Salzburg charter appears to have been copied from the one for Freising (H. Dopsch, *Geschichte Salzburgs*, p. 694). The Passau charter (Nr 306) also contained a grant of all royal rights within Passau and without, an amplification of the immunity which the bishop had received in 886 (MGH, Diplomata, Karl III, Nr 135); Salzburg's bishop likewise exercised extensive powers of immunity within the town throughout the Middle Ages and into modern times (H. Dopsch, *Geschichte Salzburgs*, pp. 681, 882-8). For the important connection between market privilege and grant of immunity see W. Schlesinger, "Der Markt als Frühform der deutschen Stadt", pp. 272-80.

[38] The confirmation of Eichstätt's privilege by Konrad I in 918 (MGH, Diplomata, Konrad I, Nr 36), but not the first grant in 908, is also preserved in the original, an indication of the unsettled political situation in post-Carolingian Bavaria (C. Hammer, *From Ducatus to Regnum*, Epilogue).

[39] See the excellent survey of Bavarian mints in H. Emmerig, "Die Münz und Geldgeschichte der Stadt Regensburg". In the early 10th century Duke Arnulf minted at Salzburg, probably because Regensburg was at that time inaccessible to him.

[40] For the use of money see C. Hammer, "Land Sales in eighth- and ninth-century Bavaria", pp. 63-66.

[41] MGH, Diplomata, Konrad II, Nr 144; this is a confirmation of a privilege granted under Otto III but the fair privilege for Donauwörth does not seem to have been included in the earlier charter.

[42] *Cartular Ebersberg*, Nr 1/3, p. 136.

[43] The account by Peter Schmid, "Die Herrschaftsträger und ihre Einflußsphären im früh- und hochmittelalterlichen Regensburg", supersedes Karl Bosl's older *Die Sozialstruktur der mittelalterlichen Residenz- und Fernhandelsstadt Regensburg*, which, nevertheless, is still worth consulting.

monastery of St Emmeram on behalf of his wife and sons who were unfree.[44] We know nothing else about Ratheri but the deed was witnessed by "the citizens of the royal borough of Regensburg" headed by Lantolt, the Under-Deputy of the City and Adelpero the Toll-Collector followed by eleven other freemen citizens as witnesses. At the same time we have evidence for a Regensburg Deputy (*vicarius*) named Polo who must have been Lantolt's superior.[45] Presumably, Polo exercised jurisdiction over a wider fiscal district around Regenburg while Lantolt and Adalpero were his agents within the city proper (or the royal portion thereof) attending to legal matters and regulation of the market. It is surely significant that these royal agents seem themselves to be accounted as members of the civic community, that is, as *cives*.

Another piece of evidence can be fitted to this deed. The first witness after Adalpero is named Odalman. In a royal charter of 893 King Arnolf granted to the nearby Bavarian abbey of Metten five plots within the city next to a tenement called Odalmann's "hovesteti" (German: *Hofstatt* or messuage).[46] This plot, identified through its tenancy by a citizen, was so prominent that it could be used in a royal document as a landmark. Like most of the early civic community, it was probably located in the area outside of the legionary fortress to the west, in the "urbs nova", also called the "pagus mercatorum" by the late 11th century, which subsequently was enclosed in the early 10th extension of the fortifications.[47] Almost a century later we learn from another royal charter of Otto II that tenants (*possessores*) of plots (*areis*) within the city of Passau paid a quit-rent (*censum*) for their properties, evidently to the king, and were seeking exemption from tolls along the waterways within the kingdom (Exhibit I.2).[48] Like Odalman these residents of Passau were probably local citizens and members of Passau's merchant community.

Just at this time towards the end of the 10th century a revealing grant to the great monastery of St Emmeram in Regensburg was executed by "a certain free and very wealthy trader of the royal borough" (*liber et predives urbis [r]egie negotiator*) named Adalhart who owned and acquired properties and slaves in a place outside the borough itself but just to the southeast and still within the comital jurisdiction (*in comitatu*) of Papo who witnessed the transaction as "borough prefect" (*urbis prefectus*), the equivalent of the "comes" in the countryside (Part II).[49] "Prefectus" was used to designate a prominent royal official, and it is likely that Papo's jurisdiction was similar to that of Polo a century earlier. Indeed, Adalhart may, like Lantolt, have served as Papo's local official, since a note added here and another deed both identify him as a "centurio" or officer responsible for the subordinate court of the hundred.[50]

The emphasis on Adalhart's free status is also significant. A contemporary royal charter of 983 confirmed a grant to St Emmeram of properties and slaves also located within Papo's "comitatus".[51] The donors were Willihalm, "our merchant" (*mercator noster*) and his wife, Heilrat. We learn from the charters that Willihalm had been "endowed with freedom" (*libertate donatus*) by Emperor Otto II's predecessors. Most likely he continued to supply the needs of the royal court, but there is no evidence that he exercised civic authority as did Adalhart. The lingering taint of Willihalm's former status with its legal disabilities

---

[44] *Trad. Regensburg*, Nr 93; for comment on the wife and children see C. Hammer, "The handmaid's tale", pp. 354-55.
[45] For these persons and matters see K. Bosl, *Sozialstruktur*, pp. 17-18; P. Schmid, "Herrschaftsträger", pp. 45-46; and now R. Deutinger, *Königsherrschaft im Ostfränkischen Reich*, pp. 56-57, fn. 11.
[46] Exhibit I.3. MGH, Diplomata, Arnolf, Nr 116: "per interventum Rihharii custodis nostril ... ad quondam abbatiunculam loco nuncupante Metamum ... perdonavimus ... urbe Radaspona curtilia quinque cum universis aedificiis iure aspicientibus ibidem prope curtem, quae dicitur Odalmann[eshovest]eti, adiacentia atque contigua, quae sunt visa esse inter conflexa duarum viarum, quae in occidentali parte praedictae curtis hoc est Odalmanneshovesteti convenient."
[47] C. Brühl, *Palatium und Civitas*, pp. 242-44, with text and comment. The term "urbs regia" which occurs in documents such as *Trad. Regensburg*, Nrs 93 and 212, may refer to this area north of the new royal palace near St Emmeram but could also have a personal sense meaning the collectivity of the civic community.
[48] MGH, Diplomata, Otto II, Nr 137; the charter is spurious but not necessarily this information. Presumably, Bishop PIigrim's intent was to eliminate royal dues and then replace them with episcopal ones.
[49] *Trad. Regensburg*, Nr 212a & b, where I take "regie" in the lower case to be "royal" rather than a form of "Regensburg". For comment on the following see P. Schmid, "Herrschaftsträger", p. 48, and Bosl, *Sozialstruktur*, p. 29; the discussion of merchants and trade in this period in K. Fischer, "Im Namen Gottes und des Geschäfts zur Stadtfreiheit", is disappointing.
[50] *Trad. Regensburg*, Nr 223. The other deeds in Adalhart's "dossier" are Nrs 213a & b, 219 and 243. Deed Nr 219 suggests that Adalhart, who had a free wife and two free sons, may have had a second family of servile origin much like Ratheri.
[51] MGH, Diplomata, Otto II, Nrs 293-96, surviving in four originals for three sets of properties; cited here from Nr 293.

excluded him from full membership in the free civic community of Regensburg[52] But it did not exclude him from judicial and commercial cooperation and personal contact with them.[53] This, however, may not have been the case for "a certain Jew named Samuhel", who owned substantial property just outside Regensburg ("in suburbano") which he had sold to the monastery of St Emmeram by 981.[54] We know that Jewish merchants were amongst those who were active as professional traders along the Danube a century earlier (below, Part I.3), and Samuhel was probably amongst their successors. While it is not certain that Regensburg was Samuhel's home, the fact that, like Adalhart and Willihalm, he too owned property near the city suggests Regensburg's importance to him.

The merchant community at Regensburg was still not a unified body at the end of the 10th century. It included diverse elements of differing status: free and unfree, Gentile and Jew. Nor did its structures comprehend the entire urban population. Nevertheless, at Regensburg by the late 9th century and at Passau by the late 10th century we have our first direct evidences for civic communities of prosperous, free traders living directly under royal jurisdiction, even acting as royal agents in local matters, and occupying important properties there as royal tenants. They did not comprise unified, autonomous communities governed by gilds merchant, much less by sworn communes, but these traders and merchants, "negotiatores" and "mercatores", clearly had high status and exercised significant authority in matters which concerned them directly. The precocity of civic development at Regensburg is underscored by the situation at Salzburg, also a notable urban settlement, where the first notices of *cives* do not occur until the 12th century; the dominant position of the Crown in Regensburg was clearly decisive for the early formation of the civic community there while the other five places remained firmly under episcopal authority.[55]

The six places in Exhibit I.1 are arranged from left to right according to my assessment of their relative "urbanity". However, it is clear from the Exhibit and from the foregoing discussion that Regensburg was "sui generis". By the late 9th century, possibly earlier, it had largely passed from its "proto-urban" stage, a development not duplicated until a century later at Passau and Salzburg with their episcopal regimes. At the other end of the scale, Eichstätt and Freising appear to have remained rather simple places throughout our period, still existing largely off their clerical establishments to which belonged most of their inhabitants. They did, however, now exercise an established central economic role for their countrysides as sites of chartered daily markets and mints. But these six places were not the only markets to which Bavarians had regular recourse.

I.3 Para-Urbanism and Marketplaces

I thought that I had coined the term "para-urbanism", but Google taught me better! It was used by the distinguished critic of urbanism, Paul Goldberger, in a 2001 speech at Berkeley.[56] By this "new urban paradigm" he means the multiple-activity centers which are located primarily, but not exclusively, in the suburbs. I here use the term in a slightly different sense to denote something which can accompany urbanism as a supplement rather than a substitute, much like para-transit fills the gaps in the public transit network. The primary urban function addressed in what follows is the market; the primary problem is to distinguish between the gaps and the fabric of early-medieval Bavaria.

---

[52] Thus, the need to travel to Verona for elaborate and expensive royal confirmation: because of his previous servile status, Willihalm continued in a state of limited dependency, and the validity of any transaction could be challenged despite the legal precautions reported by the charter. *Trad. Regensburg*, Nr 217 refers to the grant in the Nordgau by a, "servus aecclesie nomine Willihalm". Willihalm had other property in the Nordgau (MGH, Diplomata, Otto II, Nr 296), and it is possible that "servus" is to be taken here as a dependent monastic agent.

[53] *Trad. Regensburg*, Nr 243 records Adalhart's participation in a grant as "advocatus" or lay-steward of a "femina", Adalpiric, "pro eius [Adalpiric's] requie et domni sui Willihalmi". In the royal charters Willihalm and his wife expressly excluded four unnamed "mancipia" whom they retained. Adalpiric's grant was of three named, female "mancipia". Very possibly Adalpiric was the fourth: a favored slavewoman subsequently manumitted and provided for by her master, Willihalm, with Adalhart's assistance?

[54] MGH, Diplomata, Otto II, Nr 247: "quod idem [praedium] nostro permissu ex quodam Iudeo Samuhl dicto in anterius praetio [monachi] comparaverunt"; as a Jew, Samuhel was dependent on the Crown and not free to dispose of his property which came to St Emmeram in the form of an imperial grant.

[55] For Salzburg see H. Dopsch, *Geschichte Salzburgs*, pp. 681 and 687.

[56] "Cities, Place and Cyberspace", University of California, Berkeley, 1 February 2001 (www.paulgoldberger.com/speeches).

In the early 10th century Bavarian magnates brought complaints to the young (and last East Frankish) Carolingian ruler, King Ludwig IV, known as "the Child" (r. 900-911), regarding restrictions on trade in the Bavarian East. The king ordered an inquiry by the relevant marcher authorities there who took sworn evidence about conditions as far back as the reign of his great-grandfather, King Ludwig the German (r. 817/26-76). Fortunately, the results of their inquest held at the place Raffelstetten on the south bank of the Danube about halfway between the mouths of the Rivers Traun and Enns have been preserved in a 13th century copy from Passau (Exhibits I.3 and I.4).[57] It is divided into chapters in the form of a Frankish capitulary and constitutes a "Weistum" or legal precedent which could then be used for determining future disputes regarding tolls to be levied along the Danube beyond Passau: between Rosdorf, now disappeared but located upstream from Linz, and Mautern, the old, fortified Roman "civitatula" of *Favianis*, before reaching the Moravian frontier, probably near the old Pannonian provincial boundary just west of Vienna.[58]

As was customary in the early Middle Ages, the document distinguishes between two types of trade: one was "subsistence" trade which was used to obtain necessary articles for one's own consumption and which could not be produced on one's properties; the other was "commercial" trade which was carried on to enrich the trader. It also distinguishes between residents of Bavaria, regardless of ethnicity, and foreigners. In general, Bavarians engaged in "subsistence" trade were free from tolls although a charge might be levied for use of a public facility such as a highway (c. 5). It is quite clear from the document that the bulk of this "subsistence" trade was what we might also call "seigneurial" or "proprietary" internal trade where ecclesiastical establishments and lay lords sought to supply their households using both free and servile agents. But there were also professional traders for which the "Weistum" uses uniquely the term "mercatores" (c. 9), coming certainly, as we just saw in Part I.2, from places upstream within Bavaria itself such as Regensburg and Passau but also from distant places overland, perhaps even as far away as Russian Kiev.[59]

The capitulary shows clearly that this was largely commodity trade: foodstuffs, livestock, slaves, and, most prominently, salt.[60] We might expect some more exotic items amongst the unspecified merchandise, and Slavic traders seem to have had a specialization in beeswax used for church candles. The ubiquitous salt was derived from the brine-wells at Reichenhall southwest of Salzburg.[61] Although the saltworks there must originally have been a fiscal monopoly, by the 8th century rights to collect brine and facilities to render it in heating pans had been granted to a variety of ecclesiastical institutions and magnates. For the rest it was possible to buy salt directly in bulk at Reichenhall, but most consumers would probably not be able to deal with the quantities and logistics involved.

Although salt was clearly shipped overland from Reichenhall, the Bavarian salt trade seems to have favored distribution by ship, since this was probably cheaper and swifter than by cart despite the vicissitudes of seasonal water-flow and current.[62] From Reichenhall salt was sent downstream on the River Saalach, to the Salzach, the Inn and, finally, the Danube and then up the Danube's tributary streams such as the River Traun. The salt would have been unloaded at the closest river ports and then,

---

[57] MGH, Capitularia, vol. 2, Nr 253, pp. 249-52. Two studies are essential for understanding this document: M. Mitterauer, "Wirtschaft und Verfassung in der Zollordnung von Raffelstetten"; and P. Johanek, "Die Raffelstetter Zollordnung und das Urkundenwesen der Karolingerzeit". My division of the document in Exhibit I.4 differs from Mitterauer's without any claim to superiority.
[58] *Vita Severini*, Chapter Index for c. 3.
[59] The "Weistum" includes the areas along the River Rodl and in the Riedmark across the Danube to the north and northeast of Linz, which were possibly visited by traders from the Rus as well as by Bohemians for which see the differing views of: E. Zöllner, "Rugier oder Russen in der Raffelstettener Zollurkunde?"; and A. Gieysztor, "Les marches et les merchandises entre le Danube et la Volga aux viiie–xie siècles", pp. 514-18.
[60] For a useful discussions of early-medieval commodity trade see R. Hodges, *Dark Age Economics*, pp. 105, 124-29 ("utilitarian items"); and C. Wickham, *Framing the Early Middle Ages*, pp. 699-700 ("bulk exchange").
[61] H. Wanderwitz, *Studien zum mittelalterlichen Salzwesen in Bayern*, esp. pp. 209-19, is essential although the study concentrates on the high-medieval period and, in my view, underestimates large-scale trade in the early Middle Ages (pp. 216-17).
[62] The exemptions from tolls granted to the Alemannic monastery at Kempten originally covered carts sent to fetch salt at Reichenhall but subsequently for boats (MGH, Diplomata, Ludwig the German, Nrs 24 and 36).

if necessary, brought inland by cart and pack-horse.[63] The Raffelstetten inquest identifies markets held at Rosdorf, Linz, Ebersburg and Mautern along the Danube, "or wherever else a salt market might be established at that time" (c. 7). These markets were subject to comital oversight and regulation (*bannum comitis*) although at Mautern this excluded the power – apparently, exceptionally – to fix prices for salt (c. 7). Goods other than salt were evidently also offered for sale at these salt markets.

In the introduction to this chapter (Part I.1) it was argued that "proto-urbanism" was severely attenuated on the eastern Bavarian frontier comprising the old Roman province of *Noricum Ripense*.[64] Nevertheless, the Raffelstetten Inquest shows that a well-established and regulated network of marketplaces satisfied local consumers' needs there and furthered regional and long-distance trade in other valuable commodities such as slaves.[65] These Norican marketplaces were often located at fortified sites such as the Ebers-burg and clearly display some level of continuity with Roman predecessors as did four of the six proto-urban boroughs. For example, in the "Life" of St Severin we learn that in the fifth century the barbarian Rugians held a thriving market across the Danube from Mautern.[66] Very likely, the 10th century salt market at Mautern (c. 7) was also held on the north bank of the Danube at the site of Krems/Stein, the oldest "capital" of *Ostarrichi*. Thus, these central places in the Bavarian East represent, in some respects, only a difference in degree from the proto-urban settlements of the western Old Bavaria. Perhaps, the most striking divergence between them is the complete absence in the East of cathedral establishments and the paucity of important monastic foundations there, both of which played such a critical role in shaping early urban development to the west. Rather, for these eastern sites it is primarily their economic role as marketplaces and secondarily their function as royal administrative centers which stand out most clearly in the surviving documentation.

Did such marketplaces also exist in western Old Bavaria between the Rivers Lech and Inn? Here our primary sources of detailed economic and social evidence, the episcopal cartularies from Freising, Regensburg and Passau, leave us in the dark as they do on the urban structures and communities of their episcopal seats. However, if we take our clues from the Raffelstetten Inquest, then we will look for certain promising characteristics of "para-urban" marketplaces. In the first place, they will certainly be sited along navigable rivers or major roads. Second, they probably will be under royal authority and possibly located on fiscal properties.[67] Third, salt coming from Reichenhall by boat or road will likely be the basic commodity and commercial core around which such regular markets will be organized throughout Bavaria.[68]

Bavaria between the Rivers Lech and Inn, the heart of the old Bavarian duchy, was drained by the River Isar and its tributaries. However, although the Isar and its tributaries were to some extent navigable

---

[63] These river ports could also be valuable fiscal monopolies. See Ludwig the Child's 904 grant to St Emmeram of a small property on the west bank of the lower Inn, previously attached to the "curtis" of Muning, where the "port called Malching" was established at the mouth of the River Marlupp together with the concession of "portaticum" collected there (MGH, Diplomata, Ludwig the Child, Nr 30; for the numerous fiscal estates in this area including Muning see MGH, Diplomata, Karl III, Nr 128).

[64] The absence of any direct reference to a market at Lorch, only to the highway crossing at the River Enns (c. 5), is particularly striking. With the remains of its legionary fortress it was, like Regensburg, still an important site. Charlemagne used it as his advanced operational base against the Avars in 791 where he established camp, "in tabernaculis prope oppido nuncupante Loriaca" (*Trad. Freising*, Nr 143, p. 148), and Lorch is mentioned in 805 along with Regensburg as one of the frontier stations where attempted arms shipments by traders (*negotiatores*) to the Slavs and the Avars were controlled by the relevant imperial *missi* (MGH, Capitularia, vol. 1, Nr 44, c. 7). For its late-Carolingian successors, the monastery of St Florian and the Ennsburg, see the remarks in H. Wolfram, *Die Geburt Mitteleuropas*, pp. 226-27.

[65] For the slave trade see now M. McCormick, "New Light on the Dark Ages; How the Slave Trade Fuelled the Carolingian Economy", pp. 40-54, with a rare and fleeting reference to the Raffelstetten Inquest on p. 44, fn. 62; C. Hammer, *A Large-Scale Slave Society of the Early Middle Ages*, pp. 53-55. The evidence of the capitulary would be consistent with a slave trade down the Danube and directly to Constantinople rather than over the Alps and through Venice but see A. Gieysztor, "Les marches et les marchandises", p. 516.

[66] *Vita Severini*, c. 7/4: "nundinis frequentibus"; dc. 9/1: "transvadare Danuvium ... in nundinis quaereret barbarorum".

[67] As Michael Mitterauer showed very clearly, market districts in the East were allocated by comital jurisdiction, but that neat arrangement might not be so distinct in the older-settled lands of the West whose organization long predated the introduction of the Frankish comital system under Charlemagne ("Wirtschaft und Verfassung", p. 242; cf. H. Wanderwitz, *Salzwesen*, p. 216).

[68] For salt as, "ein charakteristisches Gut des permanenten Marktverkehrs", see M. Mitterauer, "Jahrmarktkontinuität und Stadtentstehung", pp. 177-78.

on a seasonal basis, it could not support the intense traffic of the Inn with its larger alpine watershed. Moreover, this part of Bavarian *Raetia* was, as we have seen, notably deficient in ancient urban centers. Still, it was crossed by several major Roman highways. The most important of these East-West routes in Roman times led directly across the Bavarian piedmont from Norican *Iuvavum*/Salzburg to Raetian *Augusta*/Augsburg. However, not all of this route, particularly in the west, was fully usable for long-distance travel in the later Roman period or early Middle Ages. Rather, the main route from Salzburg to Augsburg now took a turn to the north at the River Inn or further west at (Klein-) Helfendorf (Roman *Isinisca*) until it reached a more northerly East-West road coming from Lorch and Wels in *Noricum* (joined by another from Passau) which crossed the Isar at Föhring, now Oberföhring, an eastern neighborhood of Munich on the right bank of the river.[69] About 20 kilometers east of Föhring another North-South road branched off to follow the course of the River Sempt, a southern tributary of the Isar, north to an intersection southeast of Freising with still another East-West road coming from Augsburg which then crossed the Isar and proceeded northeast along its left bank. This well-defined topographical landscape, bounded by the Isar on the west and north and by the Ebersberger forest on the south and centered along the north-south axis of the River Sempt, was also a well-defined historical landscape: the Sundergau.[70] Its most notable feature was an exceptionally-thick concentration of ducal, then royal fiscal estates of which Föhring was one.[71]

Indeed, Föhring's name derives ultimately from an early-medieval *genealogia*, the "Ferings", and its eponym named "Fara", who were closely tied to the ducal *genealogia* of the Agilolfings.[72] Like all ducal estates, Föhring passed into the Carolingian fisc following Charlemagne's annexation of Bavaria and deposition of the Agilolfing ducal line there in 788/94. A sign of Föhring's exceptional importance is the fact that it was one of the few places in Bavaria to have a "cappella" or royal chapel, dedicated to St John the Baptist, which had passed, despite royal opposition, into the possession of the Bishop of Freising by 822.[73] The balance of the fiscal estate was granted to Freising by King Ludwig IV "the Child" in 903 to compensate for a devastating fire in the cathedral.[74] That grant tells us that Föhring, like other properties in the area, had been part of the queen dowager's appanage. It also indicates the presence of some exceptional services: privileged tenants, the oxymoronic "parscalchi" who may have had military duties and the "sindmanni" who were used for royal messenger service, and the render of "hengistfuotris censibus" or fodder for the army.[75] This "curtis" with its abundant appurtenances including mills was clearly an prominent fiscal center. Its location at a critical river crossing on a main road into the east made it a center for royal communications and military supply, and it also served as an important central place for regional assemblies and law courts.

Only five years earlier Ludwig's father, Arnolf, had granted the bishopric of Freising the right to transport salt from its works at Reichenhall wherever it wished by cart or boat free of all tolls and other charges or restrictions.[76] This was an unlimited right of toll-free transport and was quite different from the one granted earlier in the century to the monastery at Kempten in Alemannia which specified the precise

---

[69] For these routes see the detailed topographical analysis in K. Schwarz, *Archäologisch- Topographische Studien zur Geschichte frühmittelalterlicher Fernwege und Ackerfluren im Alpenvorland zwischen Isar, Inn und Chiemsee*, pp. 37-44 (Römerstrasse II [N-S] and III [E-W]), which is now incorporated into the new edition of *The Barrington Atlas of the Greek and Roman World*, Maps 12 and 19 (ed. H. Bender); G. Mayr, *Ebersberg*, pp. 6-7.

[70] The classic study of this region in the early-medieval period, albeit with genealogical focus, is Josef Sturm's, *Die Anfänge des Hauses Preysing*. See also G. Mayr's contribution to S. Herleth-Krentz, *Erding*, pp. 1-59; and C. Hammer, "Crowding the King", pp. 500-05.

[71] See G. Mayr in S. Herleth-Krentz, *Erding*, pp. 14-18, which, because of the *HAB* series' strict organization around modern administrative districts, omits the important estate at Aschheim now within metropolitan Munich.

[72] C. Hammer, *From 'Ducatus' to 'Regnum'*, p. 47; there has been needless confusion between the family and the place-name but there is no doubt about a connection between the two.

[73] *Trad. Freising*, Nrs 351 and 463.

[74] MGH, Diplomata, Ludwig the Child, Nr 28; confirmed by the new dynasty in 940: MGH, Diplomata, Otto I, Nr 30.

[75] For the "barschalks" who are rare but not absent in this part of Bavaria see especially, *Trad. Freising*, Nr 523b (825) which limits their "servitium" but provides that "itinera vicissim agant" (p.450), presumably in a support rather than combat capacity? See also M. Banzhaf, *Unterschichten in bayerischen Quellen des 8. bis 11. Jahrhunderts*, pp. 104-06 and *passim*.

[76] MGH, Diplomata, Arnolf, Nr 170.

number of carts or boats.[77] The potential scope of Freising's privilege went far beyond "subsistence trade". The river crossing at Föhring, accessible (under circumstances) by boat as well as by cart from Reichenhall, would have been an ideal place to exploit this privilege through large-scale commercial distribution of an essential basic commodity. At Föhring there was already a considerable, specialized seigneurial establishment set up by the royal fisc to service a heavy traffic load across the Isar. It would have been odd if no attempt were made at a very early date to exploit this advantageous situation. However, it is not until much later that we have direct evidence regarding Föhring's economic role as a marketplace.

In June 1158 the Emperor Friedrich I "Barbarossa" settled a dispute between his (half-) uncle, the great historian Otto, bishop of Freising, and the Welf Duke Heinrich "the Lion" of Bavaria.[78] The essence of the decision was that the market, bridge with its tolls, and mint previously located at Föhring were henceforth removed (*forum ... et pons ad theloneum ... ibidem non erit neque moneta*), and the bishop was to be compensated with proceeds from their counterparts established by Heinrich at Munich although the bishop could still maintain his own Freising mint at his discretion (*ad voluntatem suam*). The circumstances surrounding the removal of these valuable institutions to Heinrich's entirely new foundation slightly upriver on the opposite, west bank at Munich are described in a later charter issued in 1180 by Friedrich after the mighty Welf's downfall.[79] There we learn that Heinrich had "destroyed" (*destruxerit*) the market and bridge at Föhring and "transferred them by force" (*violenter transtulerit*) to Munich. Although Freising's rights were restored, Munich continued to function as the primary Isar crossing and economic center of the region while Föhring languished into modern times as a minor rural episcopal estate.

The 1180 charter maintains that Freising "had for a long time in the past quietly possessed" (*a longe retroactis temporibus quiete possederat*) market and bridge at Föhring, but we do not know precisely how long. King Konrad II's confirmation of Freising's privileges in 1029 (but not Otto I's confirmation of 940) adds a new appurtenance provision for "toll bridges" (*pontibus vectigalibus*) which probably refers to Föhring.[80] The salt traffic from Reichenhall – referred to indirectly in 1158 as the "tributum salis" at Munich to be shared with the bishop – already channeled steady traffic through Föhring. A bridge was not absolutely necessary, since the Isar could be forded there except during exceptionally high water.[81] However, the bridge would encourage additional traffic to the market, and the bridge-tolls mentioned in Konrad's confirmation would make a bridge an even more attractive financial proposition for the bishops. Possibly, the original market and, more particularly, the mint to supply it with specie were erected on the basis of Otto III's original grant of 996 even though that charter specifies their establishment "in loco Frigisinga". However, a certain discretion regarding location seems to be indicated by the charter of 1158, and medieval people, like modern people, did not always wait for official authorization to do what made good economic sense.

One of the petitioners named prominently in King Ludwig's 903 grant of Föhring to Freising was a "comes" or royal sheriff, Sigihard. As we shall see in Part II, this royal official had been active in Bavaria in the later 9th century under Ludwig's father, King Arnolf, and grandfather, King Karlmann, and had received important grants of property from the former.[82] In 888 he received full hereditary ownership (*in*

---

[77] Six carts or three boats, an interesting indication of relative capacity (MGH, Diplomata, Ludwig the German, Nrs 24 and 36)! The peculiarity of this privilege can be inferred from A. Stoclet, *Immunes ab Omni Teloneo*, p. 338.

[78] MGH, Diplomata, Friedrich I, Nr 218. A major scholarly conference ("München, Bayern und das Reich im 12. und 13. Jahrhundert") to celebrate the 950th anniversary of this charter, the first document to mention Munich, was held there in March 2008 and summaries of the papers are available at the website: www.hsozkult.geschichte.hu-berlin.de/tagungsberichte/id-2069. Of particular interest here are those by Christine Rädlinger on the topographical situation and Gertrude Thoma on the relevant privileges of the Freising bishops (see below); the complete papers have now been published in *München, Bayern und das Reich im 12. und 13. Jahrhundert*, which I have not been able to consult.

[79] MGH, Diplomata, Friedrich I, Nr 798.

[80] MGH, Diplomata, Konrad II, Nr 136, which quotes the relevant charters of 898 and 903. See the summary of Gertrude Thoma's paper (above, fn. 78); the establishment of new markets within the diocese was forbidden in 1140.

[81] Summary of C. Rädlinger's paper (above, fn. 78).

[82] For Sigihard and the Counts of Ebersberg see below, Part II.4-8 and the valuable studies by W. Störmer, *Adelsgruppen im früh- und hochmittelalterlichen Bayern*, pp. 165-75; G. Flohrschütz, *Der Adel des Ebersberger Raumes im Hochmittelalter*,

proprietatem) of a chapel (*cappellam unam*) and the attached manorial estate (*curtis*) at "Pergon" which previously he had held as a benefice (*in beneficium*) from the royal fisc.[83] In 896 Sigihard received an additional royal grant in Bavaria: three hides each at Kaging and Wörth.[84] Wörth is located in the valley of the river Sempt along the route going north from the East-West road to Föhring; Kaging, lies only 12 kilometers southeast of Wörth at the north edge of the Ebersberger Forest and on the Föhring road itself. But there is some uncertainty about the location of the clearly more important chapel also evidently dedicated to St John the Baptist and manor at "Pergon".[85]

Luckily, we have some early testimony on this point, since Sigihard's grandson, Count Eberhard, founded the monastery of Ebersberg which came into possession of the family's property including the original royal deeds just cited. An 11th century abbot there, Williramm (1046-1085), memorialized the family and their benefactions in two ways: he created a cartulary which recorded their grants and a chronicle which recounted the early history of the foundation.[86] In the chronicle Sigihard is described as a "preses" or sheriff, "who held the royal market (*fiscale forum*) at the trading sites (*secus emporia*) on the River Sempt whence the same name of the place is derived".[87] In the cartulary the first property listed is Count Eberhard's "fiscal estate (*fiscalem curtem*) which is called 'at Sempt'".[88] The only place to which the chronicle and the cartulary can both be referring as "Sempt" is the "Pergon" with its valuable chapel and estate granted to Sigihard in the charter of 888.

But this does not locate the place precisely. Several small streams now comprise the headwaters of the Sempt south of the modern town of Markt Schwaben. The East-West road from Kaging to Föhring skirted them passing through the nearby hamlet of Niederried where the North-South route heading up the Sempt valley towards Wörth crossed it. Thus, Sigihard's "forum fiscale" and the "emporia" were probably located near the source of the River Sempt and close to a major cross-roads. He thus controlled the road system in this area.[89] Sempt, at the very center, occupied a highly-accessible market location and lay about a full day's journey by cart from the nearest (known) competition at Föhring! Indeed, the parallel to Föhring with its own chapel, "forum", and fiscal estate is striking. Abbot Williramm or his scribe was probably introducing a verbal anachronism when he also called Sigihard's establishment a "forum", a term for marketplace which began to replace "mercatus" only from the 10th century, but there is no reason to doubt the accuracy of his report.[90]

Föhring and Sempt were not precisely Old Bavarian counterparts to the marketplaces at Rosdorf, Linz, Ebersburg and Mautern described in the Raffelstetten Inquest for the colonial East which had far older roots and (evidently) wider economic influence. But their functions as regional distribution centers were quite similar. Föhring with its bridge and mint appears to have been the more substantial place although that may be an illusion of the documentation. Certainly, the "forum" at Sempt served a prosperous market hinterland including the rich estates of the Sundergau. Otherwise, the two places are remarkably similar: both originally fiscal properties with chapels dedicated to St John the Baptist, both located on a major salt route, and both apparently serving as regional marketplaces although we cannot specify the precise dates when they assumed that role. Both of them had resident populations – perhaps, in the low 100s – on their estates which could service the needs of travelers passing through and of merchants coming periodically to trade – but how often and in what variety we do not know. It is true that these

---

and G. Mayr, *Ebersberg*, pp. 95-115.
[83] MGH, Diplomata, Arnolf, Nr 5.
[84] MGH, Diplomata, Arnolf, Nr 144.
[85] For the chapel's dedication see G. Mayr, *Ebersberg*, p. 48.
[86] *Cartular Ebersberg*; *Chronicon Ebersbergense*, pp. 9-16; see below, Part II.4.
[87] The *Chronicon*, p. 10, adds that Sigihard also received three hides each at Kaging and Ötting, the latter adjacent to Wörth, so clearly the charter of 896 is being cited here and the place-name has "wandered" as often happened in the early Middle Ages.
[88] *Cartular Ebersberg*, Nr I/2, p. 134.
[89] In view of the concentration of Roman artifacts in this area, one may wonder, as Paul Reinecke speculated, whether this was the site of the otherwise-unidentified Roman *Turum* mentioned only in the "Antonine Itinerary" rather than the conventional location proposed further east by Haag (P. Reinecke, "Turum, Iovisura, Patrensibus, Sorviodurum, Augustis", p. 61; G. Mayr, *Ebersberg*, p. 7).
[90] For the use of "forum" and its relation to early-medieval urban development see W. Schlesinger, "Der Markt als Frühform der deutschen Stadt", pp. 283-91, with reference to Föhring there on p. 285.

were servile populations belonging to their respective seigneuries, but, as we saw at Föhring, they were not undifferentiated. Populations of seigneurial dependents continued to comprise the majority of inhabitants at our "proto-urban" places as well for some time.

I.4 A Two-Tiered Urban Landscape

Six "proto-" and about the same number of "para-"urban places; not much of a tally for a country as large as early-medieval Bavaria. If, for example, we look at early-medieval England from York southwards, we will find (depending upon precise definition and date) perhaps as many as 40 places with a claim to at least some degree of "proto-urbanity" in an area only about one-third larger than Bavaria north of the Alps.[91] But, while there are no additional candidates for the "proto-urban" list, we may be quite confident that our "para-urban" count is far too low. If we consult the *Historical Atlas of Bavaria*'s map of "Towns and Markets in the Middle Ages", it appears to confirm our original assertion about a certain "urban deficit" in Bavaria in comparison with Franconia or even Swabia.[92] But it also witnesses to vigorous urban expansion under the Wittelsbach dukes who succeeded to the duchy in 1180 and pursued an aggressive policy of chartering new towns. One of them was Markt Schwaben (by 1310), probably the successor to early-medieval "Sempt", whose (continued) designation into modern times as a "Market" is a peculiarity of Bavaria and Austria. Thus, not all new towns would have been entirely new; there were clearly old, established bases on which to build both in Old Bavaria and in the new Austria.

We may suspect then that Old Bavaria was covered by a network of marketplaces much like Föhring and Sempt which have, unfortunately, remained largely undocumented. There were many fiscal estates, and salt, the commercial nucleus around which these marketplaces were organized, was a necessity everywhere; indeed, salt was evidently the very basis of the regional-trade and local-commercial networks in early-medieval Bavaria.[93] Although some slaves were undoubtedly traded locally at the para-urban marketplaces of Old Bavaria, I suspect these places lacked the long-distance function and exotic international flavor of their eastern counterparts described so-vividly in the Raffelstetten Inquest with what appears to be their large-scale export trade in slaves. Similarly, these "para-urban" marketplaces in Old Bavaria probably operated at a level below the larger "proto-urban" towns with regard to the complexity of their economic organization and the scope of their regional impact. Still, a well-established regional marketplace such as Föhring with a multiplicity of functions must have rivaled a smaller episcopal borough such as Freising. After all, it was attractive enough to cause Duke Heinrich the Lion to "market-nap" it for his new foundation at Munich!

Still these provincial marketplaces were not (quite) comparable – despite Abbot Williramm's description of Sempt – with the thriving "emporia" which early-medieval archaeology has revealed in northwestern Europe at places such as Dorestad and Quentovic.[94] Our Bavarian "para-urban" marketplaces were, in Richard Hodges' terms, Type A settlements, "administered periodic market-places", in contrast to the early Type B "emporia" under royal authority which were, "permanent settlements often with gridded streets, and accommodations for large numbers of craftsmen ... centres of monopolistic regional production, albeit distinctive for their involvement in long-distance trade." Such exotic places, powerful international economic centers but with very attenuated political and ecclesiastical structures and authority, did not exist anywhere in early-medieval Bavaria, and they were succeeded elsewhere around

---

[91] See the map on p. 43 and the Tables on pp. 748-53 in *The Cambridge Urban History of Britain*.
[92] *Bayerischer Geschichtsatlas*, Map 22a (Städte und Märkte im Mittelalter) with commentary by S. Hiereth and G. Diepolder on pp. 81-83.
[93] Whether Sempt was the site of a "staple" as suggested by Gottfried Mayr is possible but not certain; the importance of salt, however, is signaled by the name of the road leading from Ebersberg to Sempt, the "Halweg" (*halwec*) (G. Mayr, *Ebersberg*, p. 47; *Cartular Ebersberg*, Nr 1/35). The distribution of salt from a limited number of production sites in northwestern Europe was widely privileged by the Crown and formed the basis of regional trade networks elsewhere in *Francia*; see Map 5 in A. Stoclet, *Immunes ab Omni Teloneo*, pp. 500-01; and C. Wickham, *Framing the Early Middle Ages*, pp. 799-801; John Maddicott, "London and Droitwich, *c.* 650-750", provides a contemporary English counterpart.
[94] R. Hodges, *Towns and Trade in the Age of Charlemagne*, pp. 76-92; C. Wickham, *Framing the Early Middle Ages*, pp. 681-88.

800 by towns very similar to Regensburg, Passau and Salzburg which were combined centers of lordship and commerce.

Paul Goldberger refers to modern "para-urbanism" as "pseudo-urbanism": the city with its urban grit and diversity removed and made safe and sanitary for suburbia. All early-medieval towns retained a certain rural character, but Föhring and Sempt, both established upon rural estates where cultivation and grazing still flourished, were undoubtedly less differentiated from their surrounding countrysides than were the six Old Bavarian boroughs. Most visibly, they lacked impressive fortifications and monumental buildings. But they were not "pseudo" anything. They were quite clearly a distinct form of economic organization adapted to the needs of their society.

Bavarian boroughs were few and far between, and these established rural marketplaces supplemented urban offerings until they were replaced in the high and late Middle Ages by chartered communities with distinctly urban characteristics. Such a "two-tier" system of proto-urban centers and para-urban marketplaces is detectable also in Anglo-Saxon England, and I suspect that for most early-medieval Bavarians (as for most "Old English") – certainly for the unfree mass of the population – these para-urban marketplaces were the primary centers of economic exchange and social intercourse while the boroughs existed primarily as centers of lordship and commerce to serve the interests of the powerful and well-to-do.[95] Thus, in a very real sense, these marketplaces were the basic fabric of the commercial economic landscape, and the towns merely filled in the gaps.

---

[95] See the discussion by Grenville Astill in *The Cambridge Urban History*, pp. 27-49, here: pp. 33-37.

Part II. From Sheriff to Count: Comital Government and the Feudal Transformation in Early-Medieval Bavaria

Comital Structures and Personnel in Carolingian Bavaria

II.1 Early Carolingian Comital Rule: The Regime of Audulf:

Einhard's "Life" of Charlemagne tells us that after the deposition of Charlemagne's unruly first cousin, Duke Tassilo, in 788, the governance of Bavaria was "committed to the rule of *comitibus*".[1] These officials – the *comites* – were the everyday workhorses of Carolingian administration, responsible amongst other things for holding courts, mustering troops, and overseeing fiscal estates, regalian rights, and other crown properties and prerogatives.[2] But Einhard had something quite different in mind. He overlooked contemporary reality – the establishment in Bavaria of the first Carolingian royal regime east of the Rhine – and recalled the great Bavarian "proconsuls" of the late eighth century: first Charlemagne's brother-in-law, Gerold, and, after his untimely death in 799, a dual regime. The western lands which had been part of Bavaria since early-Merovingian times – here called "Old Bavaria" – were governed by the former royal seneschal, the *comes* Audulf; the newly-established eastern March, extending east from the river Traun and composed of recently-conquered territories was ruled by the *comes* Cotahram and his successors. Nevertheless, Einhard's point is basically correct. The full introduction of a Carolingian comital regime did not take place in Bavaria until after the "Anschluss" of 788. Thanks to the many deeds in Bavarian cartularies – particularly the great collection from the western bishopric of Freising – we can describe in remarkable detail the structure and identify the personnel of this essential instrument of Carolingian rule.

The Latin word "comes" in early-medieval sources is invariably translated into English as "count", but I believe this is misleading.[3] Generally, in modern usage the title "count" is a personal title denoting very high aristocratic status and commanding extensive proprietary resources; the modern English equivalent is "earl". While any prominent early-medieval royal official would be a person of some personal means and authority, there was no assurance that the *comes* in Carolingian Bavaria was even the strongest member within his jurisdiction, his *comitatus*, since the Bavarian Law Code foresaw that he might not be able without higher assistance to discipline all of its participants on campaign (Title 2/5).[4] Moreover, the term "count" has dynastic connotations and implications of autonomous – even autogenous – authority which, as we shall see, are inappropriate for Bavaria in the early ninth century. The term "sheriff" better captures the essential nature of the Carolingian *comes* there as a royal official owing his office to the ruler from whom he ultimately derived his authority.

In fact, the best-known witness to this conditional status is an often-cited Bavarian deed of 814 (Exhibit II.1).[5] There the "comes" Orendil conveys property to Freising for the salvation of his own soul and his kin. Orendil reserved seisin to himself during his lifetime and further stipulated that, "if any of my sons might be so worthy that he should attain to the office of *comes*", that son should receive the property in benefice from the bishop. But "worthy" (*dignus*) in what sense? Clearly, on the one hand the ruler and the high royal officials such as Audulf and the bishops who exercised immediate authority in Bavaria on his behalf would need to consider the man trustworthy and capable of carrying out his duties. This

---

[1] *Vita Karoli*, c. 11. For the following see C. Hammer, *From Ducatus to Regnum*, pp. 135-36, 248-62.
[2] The voluminous older and somewhat esoteric German literature on the "Graf" and "Grafschaft" is reviewed conveniently in E. Hlawitschka, *Vom Frankenreich zur Formierung der europäischen Staaten- und Völkergemeinschaft*, pp. 182-85, with bibliographical references. For later Carolingian East Francia there is now a thorough but somewhat agnostic review in R. Deutinger, *Königsherrschaft im Ostfränkischen Reich*, pp. 146-65. For Carolingian Bavaria the best modern account is in W. Störmer, *Früher Adel*, pp. 392-414. Michael Borgolte's two studies of comital structures and prosopography in neighboring Alemannia remain the best regional accounts for this period: *Geschichte der Grafschaften Alemanniens in fränkischer Zeit*; and *Die Grafen Alemanniens in merowingischer und karolingischer Zeit*.
[3] So, for example, David Ganz in his excellent new translation of the *Vita Karoli* (*Two Lives*), p. 26: "entrusted to counts."
[4] Text of the Bavarian Law Code: *Lex Bav*, Titles 2/5 and 2/14, respectively. In its surviving form, the Code was redacted under Charlemagne and which continued to be copied and applied throughout the early Middle Ages as we shall see in Part II.8.
[5] Comment in R. Deutinger, *Königsherrschaft*, p. 157.

would require sufficient judgment, proprietary resources, and status amongst his fellows to command their respect and, when necessary, their obedience.

In early-medieval society these necessary qualities were all associated with noble birth. By his gift Orendil created an endowment for the office, free of family claims, and an inducement for his sons to emulate his own career. But still there was no certainty – only a pious hope – that any of them would be likewise honored with his royal office. Nevertheless, kinship must have played some role in comital appointments. Very recently Erwin Kupfer has identified three possible instances of succession to comital office in the early ninth century, the most convincing of which is from Sheriff Liutpald to Sheriff Ratolt.[6] But in none of these cases is a tie of kinship documented. Liutpald, however, may have been related to an earlier sheriff, Cundhart, directly or – more likely – through Cundhart's wife.[7] A similar, distaff connection, may have existed between Sheriff Job and Sheriff Alprat.[8] It is also likely that the Sheriff Drudmunt, who makes a unique appearance at Ötting in 806, was the son of Sheriff Droant, but it is not at all certain that his office lay in Bavaria.[9] Clearly there were other considerations besides descent at work under Charlemagne and his immediate successors. At the end of this Part, we shall try to determine whether there was a significant shift towards heritability during the later years of Carolingian rule in Bavaria or thereafter.

For most ninth-century Bavarians, comital courts constituted the essence of government by sheriffs. But the Bavarian Law Code, redacted in its present form under Charlemagne but containing much earlier legislation, is surprisingly silent on the sheriff's office. It has a lot to say about an official peculiar to Carolingian Bavaria, the *iudex* or justice, who appears to have been a high ducal official in pre-Carolingian administration, but under the Carolingians those officials whom we find designated as "justices" were subordinate to the sheriffs.[10] The Law Code, itself, in the second of only two references to the sheriff describes – with Carolingian emendations – the functioning of the regular comital court (Exhibit II.1). It was summoned by the appropriate *iudex*, perhaps the "resident" legal expert to the sheriff, who, in turn, was to provide a written copy of the Code, surely, an explicit reflex of c. 26 of the great "Programmatic Capitulary" of 802 (see below). Both officials evidently rendered judgment and shared the proceeds. This is an authentic witness to practice: the oldest – and heavily used – manuscript copy of the Code evidently belonged to the retinue of an early-ninth-century sheriff named Reginperht.[11]

Erwin Kupfer has mapped the occurrences of such courts in the diocese of Freising during the first half of the ninth century.[12] Aside from the episcopal seat at Freising, he has identified possibly four to six topographical jurisdictions, centered upon fiscal estates, and lying about 15 to 25 kilometers from one another. A freeman owing suit in this region could easily ride to the court, attend a session, and return home in the same day. These very modest rural jurisdictions contrast sharply with the important, urban-centered comital jurisdictions which still existed west of the Rhine where ancient Roman *civitates* survived in reduced circumstances.[13] Indeed, as we saw in Part I.2, it is very unlikely that Roman Raetia II, with its lack of substantial urban settlements east of the river Lech, was ever systematically divided into such administrative and judicial districts. This circumscribed and purely rural comital jurisdiction – quite separate also from Bavaria's episcopal structure – underscores the relatively modest position of the ordinary Bavarian *comes*.[14] Likewise, Kupfer's map indicates a large zone in the southwestern portion of the diocese encompassing the Bavarian Lake District and extending across the mountains into the upper

---

[6] E. Kupfer, "Karolingische Grafschaftsstrukturen im bayrisch-österreichischen Raum".
[7] *Trad. Freising*, Nr 349.
[8] *Trad. Freising*, Nr 135.
[9] *Trad. Freising*, Nr 226.
[10] The "iudex" title in pre-Carolingian Bavaria appears to a conservative remnant of older Merovingian usage which was earlier replaced in Frankish-ruled territories by the "comes"; see: E. von Guttenberg, "Iudex h.e.comes aut grafio", pp. 109-110. Presumably, the Bavarian "iudices" under the Carolingians were similar in function to the Frankish "scabini", who, however, never occur in Bavarian documents (*cf. Trad. Freising*, Nr 514, where the term is used uniquely for a jury of sworn witnesses).
[11] B. Bischoff, *Die süddeutschen Schreibschulen und Bibliotheken in der Karolingerzeit*, pp. 249-50; a closely related manuscript has the later entry (p. 249): "Hunc comparavi libellum ... de presbytero Reginperti comitis ..."
[12] E. Kupfer, "Karolingische Grafschaftsstrukturen im bayrisch-österreichischen Raum", p. 15.
[13] For the lack of "civitates" in Bavaria see also above Part I.
[14] See below, Part II.6 for a contrast with the situation in the Alsace.

valley of the river Inn, which – apparently – was not so organized although properties there might still be subject to comital jurisdiction. This part of Bavaria coincides with an extensive area identified in some documents with the privileged *genealogia* of the Huosi (Huosigau) and may have constituted some form of immune lordship (Störmer: *Adelspagus*).[15] The only sheriff active in transactions there, Reginhart, was almost certainly a senior member of the Huosi.[16]

Since the area mapped by Kupfer omits the dioceses of Regensburg, Passau and Salzburg to the northeast and southeast, it covers possibly only one-quarter to one-third of the area governed by Audulf in Old Bavaria. Thus, we might expect Audulf's rule to require, perhaps, 15 to 25 sheriffs. This range compares well with numbers derived from a prosopographical examination of the same evidence. The virtually entire comital "team" in Old Bavaria which Audulf supervised on behalf of the emperors Charlemagne and then Louis is gathered together in the records of four extraordinary, missatical courts preserved in the Freising cartulary (Exhibit II.2):[17]

802 Regensburg, 11 June: 20 lay officials of whom 17 were *comites*

806 (Alt)ötting, 15 December: 12 lay officials of whom 10 were *comites*

822 Ergolding, 3 April / Allershausen, 31 August: altogether 19 lay officials of whom 18 were *comites*

These large, official gatherings were summoned to important fiscal estates on imperial authority and presided over by imperial *missi* or commissioners. In addition to judicial proceedings, they were places where oaths of loyalty were sworn, imperial edicts or capitularies promulgated, and administrative and legal procedure regulated. They were occasions to exchange official information and political gossip and to deliberate on matters of mutual concern. They provided opportunities to establish and cultivate political alliances, to strengthen regional solidarity, and to negotiate private settlements. Thus, they served the purposes of the Bavarian aristocracy as well as the Crown.

These documentary "cross sections" reveal a significant degree of continuity in comital government under Audulf's rule. The early-summer assembly at Regensburg in 802 was evidently held in response to the "Programmatic Capitulary" of that year.[18] It was presided over by the two lay *missi*, Audulf and his eastern colleague, Werinheri, and by three ecclesiastical colleagues, Archbishop Arn of Salzburg (perhaps, an author of the capitulary), Bishop Adalwin of Regensburg, and Abbot Deotker of nearby Frankish Herrieden. Also present were the Bishops of Freising and Passau. Thus, this great provincial assembly meeting at the capital city included all of the great lords – both spiritual and temporal – from early-Carolingian Bavaria.[19] Seventeen sheriffs were in attendance together with three justices (*iudices*) including our hopeful father, the later sheriff, Orendil. Eight of the attendees at Regensburg in 802 also appeared at the smaller gathering at Altötting four and a half years later in 806, and of the nineteen senior officials at Ergolding and/or Allershausen in 822, ten – more than half – had attended many years earlier at Regensburg, at Altötting, or at both courts. At Ergolding and Allershausen in 822, three years after Sheriff Audulf's death and one year after Archbishop Arn's decease, we still meet with the experienced comital team that had been assembled during Audulf's twenty-year tenure (*ca* 799?-819) as Carolingian proconsul in Old Bavaria. It must have been largely this same group of sheriffs that met young King Ludwig when he arrived in Bavaria to rule four years later in 826.

---

[15] W. Störmer, *Früher Adel*, pp. 382-91; see the article with map (p. 303) by L. Holzfurtner, "*Pagus Huosi* und Huosigau. Untersuchungen zur Gaulandschaft im westlichen Oberbayern".
[16] *Trad. Freising*, Nr 142.
[17] *Trad. Freising*, Nrs 183 (802), 227 (806), 463/475 (822); 463 (Ergolding) has *missi* as plaintiffs and is presided over by "coronatores viri". Exhibit II.2 does not include any officials who attended none of these court sessions. The spans indicated for the individual officials are *minima*, since the first and last documentary occurrence may not correspond to the beginning and end of their incumbencies. Moreover, where a range of dates was possible for a documented occurrence, I have taken the latest possibility for the beginning and the earliest possibility for the end of the bar chart. Finally, it must be noted that the number of occurrences varies widely for officials, and in no case is there continuous, year-by-year documentation for the bars. Thus, possible discontinuities in careers – if such occurred – are not noted.
[18] *Cf. Trad. Freising*, Nr 186.
[19] *Cf. Trad. Freising*, Nr 299.

II.2 The Later Carolingians:

Ludwig's long reign, well-established by 830 and lasting until his death in 876, marked a distinct break in the governance of Bavaria. As indicated above, Carolingian Bavaria was already divided into two large spheres of authority: western Old Bavaria and the newer colonial lands, the Eastern March. Because of the March's military nature and its conquered status, that is, its relative freedom from entrenched interests and established seigneurial prerogatives, its constitution seems to have developed on a separate trajectory from Old Bavaria.[20] And it was there, in the "Wild East" (Herwig Wolfram), that Ludwig set out to build his royal rule independent of his imperial father and his Bavarian step-mother.[21]

But Ludwig's reorganized rule was not without effect in Old Bavaria. At least two elements of the older judicial system were jettisoned during the 830s. No special imperial courts of the kind we have just examined were convened by imperial *missi* during the early years of Ludwig's reign.[22] Indeed, even earlier the imprint of the *missus* had been very light and episodic in Bavaria.[23] Ludwig made very limited use of his own royal *missi* and but the last court session with a royal *missus* in attendance occurs in 837.[24] There is no later evidence for any attempt to exercise any institutional oversight of the sheriffs. Perhaps, the new, direct royal presence in Bavaria made this seem superfluous although Ludwig and his successors did elevate certain persons to supervise their interests in Old Bavaria – with mixed success (see below). At about the same time, in 836, we find the last evidence for that uniquely-Bavarian official: the *iudex* or justice.[25] Some of these justices must have been influential magnates in their own right – witness the attendance of two or three at each of the missatical courts and the prominence of Kisalhart in 822 – and the office does seem to have been a possible stage in the comital *cursus honorum* as it evidently was for Orendil. It is not clear whether its elimination was due to efficiency, rivalry, or greed. In any event, by the late 830s comital authority, which previously had been at times subordinate to the extraordinary powers of the *missus* and shared with the *iudex*, was now entirely concentrated within the office of the sheriff. This new simplicity is in contrast to the overlapping jurisdictions which had been characteristic of the Charlemagne's judicial "system".[26]

Another royal official, the *vassus dominicus*, makes his first appearance in Bavaria at the very beginning of Ludwig's reign. These were local magnates who had been granted properties directly from the king and who were obligated – probably by (special?) oath – to provide a variety of military and administrative services in return.[27] In July 819 we find Meginhard, *vassus dominicus*, on campaign in Pannonia, and possibly about the same time another, Engilpald, was sitting under two senior *comites* at a court held in the diocese of Passau.[28] Three Bavarian court records from 822 provide 25 names of what appear to be *vassi dominici*.[29] On purely chronological grounds it is possible that several of them subsequently served – or were even serving at the time – as *comites*, but the position, like that of *iudex*, does not seem to have been a regular stop in the comital *cursus honorum*. Fichtenau, in his classic study of Charlemagne, imagined the *vassi dominici* might be employed by the king as a possible "counterweight" to the *comites* in exceptional

---

[20] For the East see M. Mitterauer's still-definitive, *Karolingische Markgrafen im Südosten*.

[21] See C. Hammer, *From Ducatus to Regnum*, Part 5 there.

[22] See the discussions in R. Deutinger, *Königsherrschaft*, pp. 165-76; and J. Hannig, "Zur Funktion der karolingische 'missi dominici' in Bayern und in den südöstlichen Grenzgebieten", who (pp. 272-73) distinguishes three periods ending in 830 although such a classification implies, perhaps, too much for the scrappy evidence.

[23] The *missi* certainly never "dominate[d] the judicial stage" in Bavaria as claimed in W. Brown, *Unjust Seizure*, p. 141.

[24] *Trad. Freising*, Nr 626. The ruler, of course, could always dispatch his personal commissioner or *missus* to investigate a matter of interest to him or at the request of local parties, but this is different from the institutional qualities claimed for the Carolingian *missus*.

[25] *Trad. Freising*, Nrs 613-14.

[26] A point emphasized by J. Davis, "A Pattern for Power: Charlemagne's Delegation of Judicial Responsibilities".

[27] There is, to my knowledge, no good, modern study of the *vassi dominici*, although much material is collected for Bavaria in W. Kienast, *Die fränkische Vasallität. Von den Hausmeiern bis zu Ludwig dem Kind und Karl dem Einfältigen*, pp. 187-93; oddly, A. Krah's extended commentary on Kienast ("Die fränkisch-karolingische Vasallität seit der Eingliederung Bayerns in das Karolingerreich", does not deal with the Bavarian material presented by him. For the reign of Charlemagne, see the remarks in F. Ganshof, *Was ist das Lehnswesen?*, pp. 149-55.

[28] *Trad. Freising*, Nr 419; *Trad. Passau*, Nr 73a/b, *cf.* 73c.

[29] *Trad. Freising*, Nrs 463, 466, 475; the complete term itself only occurs in Nr 466, Nr 463 has no explicit designation and the ascription is inferred from the sequence of names, while Nr 475 has "alii autem vasalli".

instances, but he allowed they might likewise be appropriated to comital use.[30] In any event, the institution, like the *missus dominicus*, had a short administrative life, confined in Bavaria to the earliest years of Ludwig's reign there. Although the East Frankish king certainly had vassals of his own, there is no evidence that they were employed systematically in any way to the prejudice of comital authority.[31]

These structural changes enhanced the position (and the revenues) of the sheriff. A more elusive enhancement – a reduction in the total number of sheriffs – may also have occurred under Ludwig. Attendance at our four missatical courts between 802 and 822 included a small number of sheriffs whose primary business lay elsewhere than in Old Bavaria. But we also can be quite certain that some active sheriffs were not in attendance at these sessions although we cannot be sure of the reasons. Reginhart occurs as a sheriff in 802, but was not amongst the attendees at either Regensburg or Altötting. Sheriff Job attended at Regensburg in 802 but not at the smaller assembly at Altötting in 806; his career as sheriff, however, continued at least into 819, the year of Audulf's death. In sum, we would not want to place the total number of sheriffs simultaneously active in Old Bavaria under Audulf at much less than about 20.

Young King Ludwig seems to have culled Audulf's aging team and appointed new sheriffs to ensure loyalty to his new regime. Of the sheriffs at Ergolding and Allershausen in 822, only two, Oadalscalh and Rihho, survived the 830s in office, and only Rihho appears to have held a place in Ludwig's inner council (Exhibit II.3).[32] Some of this "wastage" can be explained by old age and indisposition, but, I think, not all of it. Indeed, it would be very surprising if Ludwig had not wanted new men to support the new direction of his rule. Yet, he must have proceeded cautiously. Both Exhibits indicate that tenure as sheriff was normally very long: a typical span of almost 25 years can be documented from the Freising records.[33] We know virtually nothing about the actual mechanics and terms of appointment, for example, whether it was done by royal charter or – much more likely – by oral charge from a senior royal official at a public assembly. But, whether the original appointment was *sine die* or, on the other hand, renewed more or less automatically at the end of each (annual?) term, in practice incumbency must have begun at a relatively young age, perhaps, the mid- to late twenties, and normally lasted for the sheriff's active lifetime into his fifties or sixties.

Rather than deposing sheriffs, Ludwig seems merely to have excluded some from his court and council. This seems to have been the case for Oadalscalh and for, at least, three others present in 822 (Exhibit II.2): Engilhart, Ellanperht and Liutpald (I). Of the members of Freising's contingent at Verdun in 843 (Exhibit II.3), there is no evidence that either of the Cundpalds (I & II), Herilant, or Orendil (II) played a significant role in Ludwig's regime. They were left quietly to pursue their normal comital duties in Old Bavaria while he got on with the reconstruction of his rule in the East and, subsequently, elsewhere in Eastern Francia. Moreover, Ludwig seems to have reduced – very modestly – the overall number of sheriffs in Old Bavaria: I count, at most, 12 men active in office there in 840, the year of Louis the Pious' death. With the end of missatical courts, we lack records of any large gatherings that might serve as a check on our prosopographical assemblages. It is clear that groups of sheriffs met together from time to time as indicated in Exhibit II.3. In 900, at the very end of our period, a Regensburg deed preserves the record of an "assembly and conference of leading men (*principes*)" held at the fiscal estate of Reisbach

---

[30] H. Fichtenau, *Das Karolingische Imperium*, pp. 118-19: "Als Gegengewicht gegen die Grafen konnten im Bedarfsfalle auch die Vasallen des Königs in den einzelnen Grafschaften dienen… In Zeiten einer starken Zentralgewalt konnte diese [= die Grafen; mistranslated by P. Munz in the English edition, p. 110] aus einer solchen Einrichtung nur Vorteil ziehen".

[31] The Bavarian contingent at Verdun in 843 included seven "Friesoni vassalli dominici" (*Trad. Freising*, Nr 661). It is not entirely clear how to interpret this reference, but, since it seems to be in contrast to the following "vasalli Paldrici" [15 names], it is probably better to interpret Frieso as the name of a contemporary Bavarian magnate than as an *ethnicum*. For a very rare, later "regis vassus" see *Trad. Regensburg*, Nr 87.

[32] Exhibit II.3 includes all persons occurring as *comites* during this period; see also the explanatory footnote to Exhibit II.2 above.

[33] This is based on 14 *comites* for whom we have securely-dated first and last documentary occurences between 791 and 855, and for whom the terms calculated are, thus, *minima*. These 14 *comites* occur on average once every two years so the documentation is reasonably continuous. The average tenure is 24.1 years with a standard deviation of 8.6 and a median of 23. The longest tenure is 37 years for Rihho (819-855, inclusive) and the shortest 10 years for Ellanperht (815-824) and Kisalhart (818-827).

on the river Vils in the diocese of Regensburg, but, unfortunately, only three sheriffs witnessed the transaction.[34] The largest gathering of sheriffs known to me was held at Schönau near Passau in 890: at least six, possibly seven sheriffs from western Old Bavaria assembled there to conduct a boundary circuit of property which was then confirmed by royal charter.[35] The obvious importance of this royal transaction indicates that, if these were not all the sheriffs of Old Bavaria, they were likely the greatest magnates amongst them. Through the rest of King Ludwig's long reign (r. 817/26-876) and those of his successors in Bavaria, his son, Karlmann (r. 876-880), his grandson, Arnolf (r. 887-899), and his great-grandson, Ludwig the Child (r. 900-911), right into the early years of the tenth century we would be hard pressed to come up with more than 15 names of serving sheriffs in Old Bavaria as can be seen from Exhibit II.2, and it is unlikely that their numbers were any greater in the following century under the Ottonians.[36]

Moreover, from the mid-ninth century, their comital jurisdictions – their *comitatus* – were increasingly associated, particularly in royal charters, with a geographical qualifier and called in Latin a *pagus*, in German a *Gau*.[37] Thus, we regularly find a property identified as "in the *pago* called X, within the *comitatu* of Y". Whether this usage, clearly borrowed from diplomatic practice long established further to the West, implies that *pagus* denoted an official judicial-administrative district or was merely a topographical term for a settlement landscape is uncertain although the latter seems more likely.[38] But the term does, I think, signal an expanded scope of comital authority consistent with the reduced number of sheriffs. In the ninth century fewer than 15 *pagi* occur in the documentation for Old Bavaria. Some were very large, indeed, easily encompassing all of the small jurisdictions mapped by Kupfer. In Bavaria some of these "pagi" may have been the exclusive preserves of individual sheriffs. Nevertheless, we cannot assign each sheriff to his "gau", nor can we identify a sheriff for every "gau". However, even if "comitatus" and "pagus" were not coterminous, we may yet perceive in this fusion of the judicial with the topographical term a further "territorialization" of the sheriff's personal authority and the establishment of an extensive comital lordship. But such a process was far from complete in ninth-century Bavaria.

Of the half-dozen sheriffs assembled at Schönau in 890 the one mentioned first in order of precedence was Engildeo (II). Wilhelm Störmer has shown how Engildeo controlled an extensive lordship in northwestern Bavaria centered on Regensburg which comprised Engildeo's own properties there, supplemented by the offices he held, first as a sheriff in the Donaugau south of the great river, and then, more importantly, as the marcher lord of the frontier Nordgau to the north.[39] Engildeo's position far exceeded that of any other sheriff in western Bavaria to the extent that King Arnolf regarded him as a threat. Engildeo even formed an incautious alliance – perhaps, a liaison – with Arnolf's aunt, the princess royal, Hildegard, and in 895 this "overmighty subject" was finally deposed. Engildeo's fate reprised that of Ernost (I) who had been brought to Bavaria by Ludwig the German at the beginning of his reign and who rose, also as the marcher lord of the Nordgau, to the position of *secundus a rege* and possibly – or so it was claimed – the father-in-law of Ludwig's son, King Karlmann. Ernost's deposition in 861 was noted with concern even amongst the West Frankish Carolingians.[40] Both Ernost and Engildeo seem – whether by formal grant or by personal influence – to have exercised a general authority in Old Bavaria similar to Audulf's, but these dramatic royal interventions against them were not typical of political life there. Rather, as marcher lords of the Nordgau, their fortunes conformed closely to the pattern on the

---

[34] *Trad. Regensburg*, Nr 178, cf. Nr 103.
[35] MGH, Diplomata, Arnolf, Nr 75.
[36] Because the sources for the 10th century, particularly the Bavarian cartularies, are much less informative than for the 9th, it would be difficult to assemble a reasonably complete prosopography and chart comital careers with any assurance, but for the diocese of Freising see the materials assembled and discussed by Gertrud Diepolder, "Bishof Abraham von Freising und achtzehn Grafen", esp. pp. 277-78.
[37] Bavarian deeds of the 9th and 10th centuries, on the other hand, seldom use "in comitatu" and "in pago".
[38] This point is brought out well for a region where the term was much better established by M. Innes, *State and Society in the Early Middle Ages*, pp. 118-24.
[39] W. Störmer, *Früher Adel*, pp. 403-05.
[40] C. Hammer, "'Crowding the King': Rebellion and Political Violence in late-Carolingian Bavaria and Italy", pp. 526-28.

eastern Bavarian frontier where powerful marcher lords – including royal sons – sought to establish autonomous lordships, found dynasties, and defy, indeed, challenge, royal rule.[41]

Such high ambitions were alien to the ordinary sheriffs of Old Bavaria. There even the evidence for comital succession within a family continues to be exceptional. It is true, for example, that two later Orendils occur as sheriffs in the area of Ebersberg (Exhibit II.2). All three may well have been related, but – given early-medieval naming practices – direct descent is unlikely. No doubt, throughout the century some sons did follow their fathers as sheriffs, and cousinages did occupy positions vital to the interests of their families. But this is only what we might expect in a small and intensely aristocratic society where substantial family resources, influence and prestige were the leading personal qualifications for public office.[42]

II.3 Carolingian Conclusions and Ottonian Outlook:

During the long century of Carolingian rule – from the late 8th century to the early 10th – the Old Bavarian *comes* continued, despite the significant expansion of his office noted above, to be a royal servant. He served a long term but still at the king's pleasure and exercised only delegated authority: he was a "sheriff" and not a "count". This pronounced characteristic of Bavarian comital office was undoubtedly due in large measure to the fact that for the East Frankish kings Bavaria was a "core" territory where they spent much time and ruled directly without a ducal intermediary. Thus, they evidently kept very tight control over their principal administrative officers, the *comites*. But even in the troubled 10th century, when the Bavarian ducal office was reinstituted and conflicts between duke and king reemerged, the duke himself – now regularly a member of the Ottonian royal family – intervened vigorously in a quasi-royal capacity to prevent Bavarian *comites* from arrogating crown prerogatives to themselves and acting beyond their constituted authority as indicated in the Bavarian Law Code which continued to be normative throughout this period. Such strong ducal supervision in the Carolingian tradition can be seen clearly in the so-called "Constitutions of Ranshofen" which were promulgated in the early 990s at a prominent fiscal estate by Duke Heinrich "the Quarrelsome" (r. 951-995), together with, "omnium primatum tam episcoporum quam comitum".[43] A *comes* who acts unjustly, "shall have neither the favor (*gratiam*) of the duke nor his office (*comitatum*)" (c. 4). Indeed, insubordinate *comites* could even be jailed or exiled (c. 6)!

And, yet, by the end of the ninth century, a significant base clearly had been laid both in Old Bavaria and in the frontier marches for developments favorable to comital autonomy. In 1949 Philippe Dollinger in his classic exposition of, "l'évolution des classes rurales" in Bavaria from the end of the Carolingian period identified several fundamental changes in comital structure; one of them was "the formation of comital dynasties".[44] Although much of Philippe Dollinger's account has now been superseded after 60 years of intensive research, still his basic point here is undoubtedly correct. The Ranshof "Constitutions" show that *comites* could be removed – *nota bene*, for cause – by the duke, but they in no wise exclude hereditary succession to the office which was an essential precondition to dynastic formation. The earliest of these comital dynasties for which we have substantial documentation is that of the Ebersberger, so named by modern historians for their foundation of Ebersberg 30 kilometers to the east of modern Munich. We have already met the first known member and dynastic progenitor, Sigihard, who flourished in Old Bavaria under the later East Frankish kings, Karlmann, Arnolf and Ludwig, and who presided over the market at Sempt (Part I.3). Thus, the family's history provides a unique opportunity to continue our story into the less well documented 10th century.

---

[41] A. Krah, *Absetzungsverfahren als Spiegelbild von Königsmacht*, pp. 197-203, 217-19.
[42] Similar considerations in T. Kohl, *Lokale Gesellschaften*, summarizing secondary literature, p. 333: "Dass es unter diesen Umständen als Sohn eines Grafen oder Schultheißen nicht unwahrscheinlich war, selbst das Amt zu erreichen, überrascht nicht – zumal dies auch nach zeitgenössischen Vorstellungen von Erblichkeit nahelag".
[43] Older MGH edition in *Leges Baiuwariorum*, pp. 484-85, reprinted in *Dokumente zur Geschichte von Staat und Gesellschaft in Bayern*, pp. 226-27; extensive commentary with text in footnotes in S. Weinfurter, "Die Zentralisierung der Herrschaftsgewalt im Reich durch Kaiser Heinrich II", pp. 252-60.
[44] Now most readily available in the excellent German translation with the misleading title, *Der bayerische Bauernstand vom 9. bis zum 13. Jahrhundert*, pp. 53-55.

Bavaria's First Count and the "Feudal Transformation"

II.4 Abbot Williram's "Chronicle" of Ebersberg:

In the later 11th century, Williram, the learned abbot (1048-1085) of the Benedictine monastery of Ebersberg in Bavaria, wrote or caused to be written a memorial of his foundation (see Exhibit II.4).[45] As sources for this "Chronicle" he had written deeds and charters in the monastery's archive and the traditions, probably both oral and written, of his congregation and of the founding family, the mighty Counts of Ebersberg, which had only recently (1045) died out in the male line. Perhaps, it was the mixed nature of his materials which caused him to begin his story long before the establishment under the Gorze Reform of Benedictines from Augsburg at Ebersberg in 1013 and even before the establishment of the first church of canons secular there in 934. Rather, Williram began with an account of the first member of the comital family known to him, Sigihard. It was a colorful story. As we saw in Part I, Sigihard had presided since the reign of King Karlmann (r. 876-880) as the royal official, a *praeses*, presiding over the royal market at the trading sites near the source of the river Sempt.[46] But his authority probably also reached further south into the great Ebersberg Forest, since one day in autumn he was hunting at the southern edge of the forest where he flushed an enormous boar from its hiding place between a sandstone outcropping and a linden tree. Sigihard and his men were unable to kill the beast, and it returned at night for several days before finally escaping the district.

The nature of the boar's appearance and behavior were clearly remarkable, and stories began to circulate about it which Sigihard evidently tried, without success, to discount. Finally, these tall hunters' tales reached all the way to Alemannia and the Alsace far to the west, and two holy men, a well-known clerk from Hohenhöwen northwest of Lake Constance and a hermit from Strassburg, both offered their interpretations and inspired advice. They both saw the extraordinary boar as an evil spirit, possibly the devil himself, and its exorcism should begin with clearing the place and making it fit for human habitation. Of course, this site should include a church safely away from the polluted ground itself, but, moreover, fortifications should be erected there to protect against a new scourge of Huns from the East. Upon hearing this, Sigihard must have begun quickly about the work which was then finished with all signs of urgency by his nephew, Oudalric [Ulrich], in a blinding snow storm. But only the fortifications, not the church, were completed. The Emperor and East Frankish King Arnolf (r. 887-899) then, according to Williram, confirmed Sigifrid's work at Ebersberg – and implicitly his authority there – by a grant in 896 to his kinsman (*consanguineus*) of additional properties near his estate at Sempt. But the charter itself, which survived in Ebersberg's archives, makes no such reference, and, as we shall see (below, Part II.7) Williram may, have reversed the sequence in his narrative and then glossed it to legitimate the deed at Ebersberg.[47]

Williram's narrative is an aetiological story to explain the place-name, Ebers-berg or "Boar's Hill", but is it only that? He has introduced folkloristic motifs, conjectures and anachronisms, but should we consider his account only "legendary"? The prescient warning from the West about the Huns, that is the Magyars or Hungarians, was well founded. The Magyars first raided into eastern Bavaria in 900 when they crossed the River Enns. In 907 the entire Bavarian leadership, both lay and ecclesiastical, was decimated by a disastrous defeat at Pressburg [Bratislava], and the next half century saw numerous Magyar incursions until they were decisively defeated at the River Lech by Otto the Great in 955.[48] In such dangerous times fortifications, which until then had hardly existed outside the episcopal cities, were a necessity throughout the countryside. Many lay aristocrats like Sigihard used this pretext to expand their authority. But few had such close support from the king. In fact, the Emperor Arnolf and his son, King Ludwig the Child (r. 899-911), both refer to Sigihard in their charters as a "close

---

[45] *Chronicon Eberspergense*, pp. 10-12.

[46] *Praeses* is an alternative term in the early-medieval sources for *comes*. Williram's account is confirmed by the surviving original charter of Emperor Arnolf dated 1 January 888 preserved with the Ebersberg monastic archives which Williram is probably citing (MGH, Diplomata, Arnolf, Nr 5).

[47] MGH, Diplomata, Arnolf, Nr 144.

[48] See now in English: C. Bowlus, *The Battle of Lechfeld and its Aftermath, August 955*, with an idiosyncratic account of the Ebersbergers (pp. 147-54).

kinsman" [*propinquus*].[49] Yet, in spite of this prominent royal connection, nothing certain is known about Sigihard's origins nor about any other of his close kin. Such genealogical obscurity is not unique. The same is true for the most important of Sigihard's Bavarian contemporaries: the *comes* Luitpold, himself a royal kinsman and progenitor of the new Bavarian ducal line of the 10th century.[50] But this documentary silence has not prevented attempts to supply the deficiencies of our sources. Of modern historians we must name, particularly, Michael Mitterauer, Wilhelm Störmer, Günther Flohrschütz, and Gottfried Mayr.[51] Building upon their thorough and acute researches it may still be possible to cast a bit of additional light on Sigihard's origins or, at least, to provide them with a richer historical context.

II.5 Sigihard's Origins:

The most remarkable aspect of Abbot Williram's account is his reference to the prophecies of the two holy men from distant Alemannia and the Alsace, respectively, which provided the charter for building the fortifications at Ebersberg, clearly a novel and possibly a risky undertaking. Flohrschütz in his careful account of the Ebersberger lordship remarked on their significance and assigned them to "the oldest traditions preserved [*Überlieferungsgut*] at Ebersberg"; he then concluded that Sigihard was, "surely a magnate in the Duchy of Alemannia and possibly a Swabian by birth".[52] There are, indeed, several pieces of circumstantial evidence which link Sigihard to neighboring Alemannia. Although there are no records of Sigihard functioning as a *comes* there, in 898 Arnolf did grant him property in the Duriagau which lay across the River Iller in far eastern Alemannia where, presumably, Sigihard already had other properties.[53] Moreover, the name of Sigihard's helpful nephew, Oudalric or Ulrich, is characteristic of a mighty comital dynasty established on the north side of Lake Constance (not far from Hohenhöwen) and descended from a brother of Hildegard, Charlemagne's wife and progenitor of the Carolingian male line.[54] But it is the connection further west to the Alsace which is more intriguing.

Michael Mitterauer identified a later memorial entry in the great Reichenau confraternity register which seems clearly to refer to Sigihard and his family.[55] The names there are recorded under the "Nomina Fratrum de Coenobio quod Sancti Gregorii Nominatur" which is the monastery of Gregorienthal in the southern, Upper Alsace. In 898 Gregorienthal was dominated by Sigihard's contemporary, the *illustrissimus comes* Eberhard, whose comital authority was centered in the northern, Lower Alsace and the adjacent Ortenau across the Rhine in Alemannia; he seems to have had a particularly close relationship with Baldram, Bishop of Strassburg and a Bavarian.[56] Both appear to have been instituted into their positions by the Bavarian Carolingian from Carinthia, King Arnolf, at the beginning of his reign. The seat of their authority, the ancient city of Strassburg, is of additional interest because it apparently was a center of hermitical zeal. In 908 the Strassburg canon, Benno, established himself as a hermit at Meinradszelle in the wilderness south of Zurich, and he was joined there in 934 from Strassburg by Eberhard, "clerk and hermit", who became the founder of the important monastery of Einsiedeln on the site and who appears to have been a grandson of the mighty *comes* Eberhard.[57] It is not so surprising then that Sigihard in far away Bavaria received a potent prophecy from a Strassburg hermit named Gebe<u>hard</u>.

Both Sigi<u>hard</u>'s and Eber<u>hard</u>'s names also contain this relatively common second element which could indicate some relationship, for example, as brothers.[58] Moreover, the name "Eberhard" recurs

---

[49] MGH, Diplomata, Arnolf, Nrs 144, 159; MGH, Diplomata, Ludwig the Child, Nr 28.
[50] C. Hammer, *From Ducatus to Regnum*, pp. 271-81.
[51] M. Mitterauer, *Karolingische Markgrafen*, pp. 212-27; W. Störmer, *Adelsgruppen im früh- und hochmittelalterlichen Bayern*, pp. 165-75; G. Flohrschütz, *Der Adel des Ebersberger Raumes im Hochmittelalter*, pp. 96-103; G. Mayr, *Ebersberg*, pp. 96-103.
[52] G. Flohrschütz, *Adel*, p. 97.
[53] MGH, Diplomata, Arnolf, Nr 159; M. Borgolte, *Grafen Alemanniens*, p. 34, *sub* "Adalgoz".
[54] See M. Borgolte, *Grafen Alemanniens*, pp. 255-66, *sub* "Udalrich III, IV, V".
[55] M. Mitterauer, *Karolingische Markgrafen*, pp. 220-22; *Das Verbrüderungsbuch der Abtei Reichenau*, pag. LV.
[56] M. Borgolte, "Die Geschichte der Grafengewalt im Elsaß von Dagobert I. bis Otto dem Großen", pp. 36-45, and *Grafen Alemanniens*, pp. 98-99, *sub* Eberhard I; H. Hummer, *Politics and Power in Early Medieval Europe*, pp. 215-35 *passim*.
[57] H. Keller, *Kloster Einsiedeln im Ottonischen Schwaben*, pp. 13-26.
[58] See *Trad. Freising*, Nrs 605, 611.

in the second and fourth generations of Sigihard's heirs (see Exhibit II.5). It has long been suspected that the Alsacian Eberhard belonged to the old ducal family there, the Etichons, and traces of early Etichon presence are detectable in Bavaria near Sempt and Ebersberg.[59] But no certain genealogical connection to the earlier Etichons has ever been established, and "the most illustrious" Eberhard even lacks an identified father just as does Sigihard.[60] Moreover, although Eberhard benefited greatly from King Arnolf, there is no mention in the two extant royal charters where he occurs that he was regarded as a royal kinsman as was Sigihard.[61] Thus, we may suspect a tie of kinship between these two mighty, contemporary *comites* of the Alsace and Bavaria, but we are unable to specify the relationship precisely.

The region directly to the north of the Alsace provides one other clue to Sigihard's background and early career. In a deed from 764 recorded nearly a century later in the cartulary of the great monastery of Weissenburg, the donor, Albrich, is identified in the later document header as "avus Sigiharti comitis".[62] This unusual biographical reference is clearly to contemporary events in the ninth century. Weissenburg was located on the northern edge of the Alsace in the diocese of Speyer; across the Rhine was the district called the Kraichgau where in 858 a Sigihard had his *comitatus*.[63] In 861 the East Frankish *Fulda Annals* inform us that a Sigihard *comes* was implicated in a conspiracy centered around Ernst, King Ludwig the German's powerful proconsul in Bavaria (above, Part II.2); also implicated was Abbot Waldo of Schwarzach in the Ortenau to the south of the Kraichgau and opposite Strassburg. They and others were deprived of their offices (*honores*) and most retired to their private estates. The king's oldest son, Karlmann, was evidently also involved and withdrew to the eastern Pannonian and Carinthian marches of Bavaria where he expelled the royal officials and, "administered the marches through his own men (*per suos*)". The Weissenburg record was being written up in the cartulary at just this time, and the scribal note probably results from Sigihard's sudden notoriety.

Is the deposed Sigihard of 861 also the Kraichgau official in 858 and the later founder of Ebersberg whom we can first trace in Bavaria from the late 870s during the reign of King Karlmann? The narrative line is compelling. It is quite plausible that the deposed Sigihard should attempt to reestablish his private and public fortunes after 861 with Karlmann on the wild frontiers of eastern Bavaria. That would explain why Karlmann later entrusted him with the administration of an important fiscal estate in western Bavaria and why Sigihard continued to enjoy the high favor of Karlmann's son, Arnolf, and grandson, Ludwig. In 868 a Sigihard occurs amongst "many of the noble men of this country [Bavaria]" in a Regensburg deed, and two decades later a Sigihard is a prominent witness to an exchange of properties in the East which was carried out "in the presence of Duke Arnolf", that is, before Arnolf seized power and deposed his imperial uncle, Karl the Fat, in 887.[64]

The objections to identifying the three *comites* are primarily chronological. If the Albrich of the 764 Weissenburg deed was truly the deposed Sigihard's "grandfather", then it is difficult to imagine that the grandson lived on into the early 10th century as did Sigihard of Ebersberg.[65] But it is unlikely that the Weissenburg scribe of *ca* 860 had precise knowledge of Albrich's descent; more likely he was using "avus" in its alternative Classical and medieval sense of "ancestor". Similarly, if Sigihard was already

---

[59] C. Hammer, *From Ducatus to Regnum*, pp. 224-25.

[60] F. Vollmer, "Die Etichonen. Ein Beitrag zur Kontinuität früher Adelsfamilien", pp. 176-78.

[61] MGH, Diplomata, Arnolf, Nrs 24 and 88. Note, however, that Sigihard was not identified as a royal kinsman in the earliest charter extant for him (Nr 5); these silences may be conscious omissions if the relationship derived from Arnolf's mother, Liutswind, as has been suspected (see below, Parts II.5 & II.7). Like his father, Karlmann, Arnolf was evidently reluctant to draw attention to his maternal kin early in his reign because of the irregular circumstances of his mother's, marital relationship and the possible political sensitivities arising from it (C. Hammer, "Crowding the King", pp. 524-35; and see below).

[62] *Trad. Weissenburg*, Nr 193, p. 399, for properties in the Saargau in southern Lotharingia; discussion of dating in H. Hummer, *Politics and Power*, pp. 181, 195.

[63] MGH, Diplomata, Ludwig the German, p. 136. There are two other records of an *illustrem virum Sigihardum comitem* (without indication of his *comitatus*) who was a benefactor and procured royal benefits for Fulda in 856 and 858, respectively (*Codex Diplomaticus Fuldensis*, Nrs 565, 566, pp. 254-55); the dating of the MGH edition of Nr 566 (MGH, Diplomata, Ludwig the German, Nr 53, p. 72 there) is in error; this subsequently-falsified charter clearly derives from the royal assembly at Forchheim in February 858 and is anticipated in Nr 565 from the year 856 as Dronke's edition implies.

[64] *Trad. Regensburg*, Nrs 73 and 102, *cf.* Nr 86.

[65] See the chronological problems encountered by Michael Mitterauer in his explorations of Albrich's relationships on this assumption (*Karolingische Markgrafen*, pp. 214-16 with chart on p. 226).

an official in the Kraichgau by 858 (and possibly by 856) then his official career may have spanned a full half century. But if we assume that Sigihard was born in about the same year as Karlmann, around 830, then he would have been in his mid- to late-twenties at his comital appointment to the Kraichgau, a typical age in contemporary Bavaria, and in his seventies at his death.[66] This indicates a remarkably robust constitution and an unusual share of good luck, but it is still well within the boundaries of the biologically possible and the biographically plausible. None of this is conclusive but it is consistent with Sigihard's having joined the retinues of Karlmann and then Arnolf in the Bavarian East. Some claim of consanguinity would only have strengthened such ties of fidelity.

Does this all mean that Sigihard of Ebersberg was an Alsacian, or an Alemann, or even a Frank from the Kraichgau? Not necessarily. In fact, the most plausible explanation of Sigihard's royal kinship remains through Arnolf's mother, Liutswind, who certainly had her family roots planted deep in Carolingian Bavaria.[67] Still, the available evidence for this connection, essentially deeds in the Freising cartulary, is sparse and laconic. When Liutswind separated from her husband Hruodperht, presumably because of her new relationship with Karlmann, a "Sigihart" was one of the witnesses to the final property settlement in 849.[68] His role as valid witness for a kinswoman would be quite compatible with our earlier assumption that Sigihart of Ebersberg was born around 830. Likewise, when in the following year Bishop Chunihoh, the primary heir of the magnate Ratold of Daglfing, disposed of properties from his inheritance, an "Eparhart" witnessed the transaction and a "Sigahart" the investiture.[69] Ratold may have been Liutswind's father and Bishop Chunihoh her half-brother. The Emperor Arnolf's final grant to Sigihard in 898 of property in the Alemannic Duriagau had previously been held as a benefice by an "Adalgoz praefectus"; in 839 Ratold of Daglfing had a deceased brother named Adalgoz.[70] These references – like the connections to Eberhard in the Alsace – are tantalizing but inconclusive hints of a relationship.

However, there is one other possible connection between Sigihard and Liutswind. We know from two of Arnolf's charters that Liutswind held as her dowager's appanage the important fiscal estate of Erding on the River Sempt and the small abbey of St Castulus at Moosburg on the River Isar which were granted by her son upon her death to the episcopal churches of Salzburg and Freising, respectively.[71] Both places lie within an area dominated by Sigihard. From a somewhat complex deed executed at a Freising synod on 13 September 908 we learn that the *abbatiola* of Moosburg was in fact then held by the Freising suffragan bishop [*chorepiscopus*] Cowo as his own property [*propriam ... suam*] which he relinquished [*remisit*] to Freising on the condition that he receive it back as a life benefice.[72] Cowo's steward [*advocatus*] for the transaction was the *comes Sigihardus* who also prominently witnessed the deed in the company of three other well-known Bavarian *comites*.[73] This is the only appearance of a *comes* Sigihard in the otherwise very ample Freising cartulary. If this Sigihard were closely related to Liutswind, say, her brother, it is quite plausible that he might act as steward for her properties which she, as a woman (and like a cleric), could not represent in legal proceedings and that his position as steward might be continued under subsequent clerical possessors. The obvious objection is that Williram's "Chronicle" tells us that Sigihard died in 906, but that information is an interpolation from the 14th century to align the passage with the 13th century "Ebersberg Posterior Chronicle".[74] We have no contemporary account providing

---

[66] For the official spans of Bavarian *comites*, see above, Part I.1.2.
[67] Regarding Sigihard's royal connection through Liutswind see the commentary in G. Mayr, *Ebersberg*, pp. 95-96; for Liutswind's identity see C. Hammer, "Crowding the King", pp. 528-34.
[68] *Trad. Freising*, Nr 706; the properties named lie within the Sempt-Ebersberg area.
[69] *Trad. Freising*, Nr 721a/b; the properties include Eggelburg, only 2.5 km from Ebersberg (see G. Mayr, *Ebersberg*, pp.99-100).
[70] MGH, Diplomata, Arnolf, Nr 159; *Trad. Freising*, Nr 634, p. 539.
[71] MGH, Diplomata, Arnolf, Nrs 87 and 136; it is not entirely clear from the wording of these charters, particularly the later Nr 136, whether Liutswind was, in fact, dead.
[72] *Trad. Freising*, Nr 1045, which seems to cite MGH, Diplomata, Arnolf, Nr 136. For political commentary on the subsequent confirmation by the Bavarian Duke Arnulf see C. Hammer, *From Ducatus to Regnum*, p. 278; and *cf.* MGH, Diplomata, Otto I, Nr 30, for subsequent settlement of this contentious property).
[73] The first *comes* listed ahead of Sigihard, Aripo, was primarily active in the East, but the two *comites* following Sigihard in the witness list, Wetti and Wolfdregil [II], were clearly western Bavarian *comites*.
[74] *Chronicon Eberspergense*, p. 10, fn. b; *Ex Chronico Eberspergensi Posteriore*, p. 868; it is possible that his wife, Cotini, died

the year of Sigihard's death, and it is easier to make this small addition to Sigihard's biography than to identify the *comes* present at Freising in 908 with some otherwise unknown son or member of an eastern cadet line.[75]

II.6 Sigihard's Descendants at Ebersberg:

Sigihard's successors did not immediately build upon his legacy at Ebersberg. His primary (and only?) heir, Ratold, bore the same name as Liutswind's possible father and as one of the Emperor Arnolf's illegitimate sons. Ratold prudently improved the fortifications there in response to the increasing depredations by the Hungarians, but he made his distinguished career far away in southeastern Carinthia where, as was just argued, his father may also have served under Karlmann and Arnolf.[76] Williram tells about two of Ratold's sons: Eberhard who appears to have been the primary heir of Ebersberg and Adalpero about whom Williram says very little (Exhibit II.4). While improving the fortifications at Ebersberg, Eberhard had a religious vision which was interpreted for him by his chaplain, Hunfrid.[77] Thus inspired and guided by Hunfrid, in 934 Eberhard built a stone church away from the site where the boar had been flushed – just as the prophecies sent to his grandfather had specified – and which still retained pagan associations, particularly the linden tree. He then furnished it with a consecrated altar containing relics of St Sebastian and endowed it with properties although his brother, Adalpero, prevented him from adding one property at Aham on the River Inn.[78] Finally, Eberhard established Hunfrid as head of a college of secular clerics where he continued to serve until his death in 970.

Eberhard died in 959 without male heir.[79] He was succeeded by his brother Adalpero who, in contrast, had eight male heirs. Adalpero's name was borne by an earlier bishop of Augsburg (s. 887-909), the preceptor of Augsburg's most prominent bishop, St Ulrich (s. 923-973). Saint Ulrich came from a prominent but elusive Alemannic family and maintained a close relationship to the cleric and hermit from Strassburg, Eberhard of Einsiedeln.[80] Adalpero of Ebersberg must have had some connection to this prominent Augsburg bishop, who would have been quite young when Sigihard's nephew of the same name completed the original fortifications at Ebersberg: the later saint baptized the least promising of Adalpero's sons who even received the bishop's name, Ulrich, and, ultimately, Ebersberg. Abbot Williram duly emphasizes the young Ulrich's piety and ascribes a prophecy to his aunt, Willibirg, to the effect that he would complete the promised endowment of the church which had been hindered by his father, Adalpero.

Ulrich's tenure as lord of Ebersberg was marked by an important event. In 970 Archbishop Friederich of Salzburg (s. 958-991), possibly a kinsman, finally consecrated the church which until then Ebersberg's ordinary, Bishop Abraham of Freising (s. 957-994), had refused for political reasons.[81] Thus, in 1013 Ulrich's wife, Rihgart, was the first of the family to be buried "in that same fortress" and not at Freising. Ulrich too was buried there next to her in 1029. He left three sons and was succeeded at Ebersberg by Adalpero II; none had male heirs. Thus, the comital line established by Sigihard died out in its fifth generation with Adalpero II in 1045 although Sigihard's descent did continue through the daughters who

---

in 906 and that his death was subsequently ascribed also to that year.

[75] From a possible repetition in the Reichenau memorial Michael Mitterauer (*Karolingische Markgrafen*, p. 222) posits a son also named Sigihard and ignored by Williram who occurs as a *comes* in Salzburg territory also in 908 (MGH, Diplomata, Ludwig the Child, Nr 64) and in 916; he does not, however, cite the Freising deed. This is also the position of Gertrud Diepolder, ("Bishof Abraham von Freising und achtzehn Graften", p. 277, fn. 6), who, however, assumes, "daß ihm zunächst ein Grafenamt im Raum des Bistums Freising übertragen war." Even if their conjecture is correct, it would not negate the familial connection to Moosburg, since a *comes* from the Salzburggau would likely be acting as *advocatus* for Freising property by an hereditary claim. Thus, it would merely displace the argument here by a generation.

[76] M. Mitterauer, *Karolingische Markgrafen*, p. 223.

[77] Hunfrid's name is characteristic (*Leitname*) of an important Alemannic family.

[78] Possibly this unexplained act earned him Abbot Williram's later *damnatio memoriae* (see below).

[79] For the following account see Williram's *Chronicon Ebersperegense*, pp. 12-15.

[80] H. Bühler, "Die Herkunft des Hauses Dillingen", pp. 16-27; M. Weitlauff, "Bischof Ulrich von Augsburg (923-973)", pp. 79-92.

[81] Abraham was closely allied with the Bavarian ducal party in a dispute with the Ottonians whom Eberhard supported (see comment in G. Mayr, *Ebersberg*, pp. 106-07; S. Weinfurter, "Zentralisierung der Herrschaftsgewalt im Reich", pp. 250-51).

had married into several distinguished families.[82] The family and their retainers left a rich legacy to the church at Ebersberg which is recorded in the monastic cartulary which also was compiled under Abbot Williram.[83]

II.7 Sigihard and the "Feudal Transformation":

Was Sigihard still a "sheriff" in the form which had evolved over the century of direct Carolingian rule in Bavaria or had he now become a "count"? That is: did Sigihard merely exercise delegated, non-hereditary authority as a royal official or was his position now based upon autonomous and hereditary authority, whether ultimately autogenous or usurped? This biographical issue is linked to a larger and very controversial historiographical debate developed largely by French historians from French sources. The "feudal transformation", which they trace from the later 9th into the 11th centuries, refers in essence to the transfer of "public" authority into "private" hands and the establishment of feudal dynasties which ruled over largely-autonomous lordships and exercised extensive governmental powers independent of and even in opposition to the king.[84] German historians have been largely absent from this debate, and German history has largely been ignored.[85]

No doubt Abbot Williram, viewing developments through his late 11th century spectacles, regarded Sigihard as a Count, and we have been describing Sigihard's descent from Williram's later perspective of male primogeniture. For Williram and his contemporaries, all of them were Counts, though not necessarily "of Ebersberg".[86] In fact, their comital status was even ascribed to the women. An Ebersberg calendar with 11th and 12th century necrological notices of comital and other benefactors also provides the death days of all of the wives and of Ulrich's daughter, Willibirg II, where they are described – uniquely – as *comitissa*, that is, "countess".[87]

Whatever, the later convention may have been, this is certainly a surprise for Sigihard's wife, Cotini, who died on 20 December, possibly in 906. We would expect only "coniunx/uxor comitis" as is usual in the Ebersberg "Chronicle" and the "Cartulary". For her, this designation as "countess" is clearly an anachronism, but not necessarily so for the entries from later in the 10th century when the titulature and possibly the position of the comital consort clearly experienced an elevation elsewhere in Europe.[88] But even if Cotini were not a "countess", she nevertheless may have played an important, even crucial role in Sigihard's career. Several of the wives must have been important actors independent of their husbands as certainly appears to have been the case with Ratold's daughter, Willibirg I. And they could be entrusted with important responsibilities: according to the Cartulary, Count Adapero II – apparently before retiring

---

[82] See the chart in G. Flohrschütz, *Adel des Ebersberger Raumes*, p.121.

[83] *Cartular Ebersberg*, pp. 115-96; see now the excellent map of Ebersberg family properties in W. Störmer's recent essay, "Hochmittelalterliche Adelsfamilien: Probleme, vor die uns die Quellen Stellen", p. 13, which also includes the later monastic foundation in northwestern Bavaria, Geisenfeld, but which eliminates nearby Kühbach, the traditional ascription of which to a cadet line of the Ebersbergers is doubtful (G. Mayr, "Die Grafen von Kühbach und ihr Verwandtschaftskreis", pp. 123-24).

[84] I here use a term coined by Jean-Pierre Poly and Eric Bournazel in their book: *La mutation féodale X^e –XIIe siècle*, here cited from the English translation of 1991: *The Feudal Transformation 900 – 1200*. For a concise and useful summary of the ensuing debate from one of the participants see now C. Wickham, *The Inheritance of Rome; A History of Europe from 400 to 1000*, pp. 508-28.

[85] See the review of the debate by a very knowledgeable historian of early-medieval Germany, the late Tim Reuter, "Debate: The 'Feudal Revolution' III", esp. pp. 187-91; and, for (counter) example, the very different recent accounts by T. Bisson, *The Crisis of the Twelfth Century; Power, Lordship, and the Origins of European Government*, and D. Barthélemy, *The Serf, the Knight and the Historian*. Bisson, in fact, makes the incredible statement (*op. cit.*, p. 119), "that we know next to nothing about lay lordship there [in Bavaria] in the eleventh century."

[86] See W. Störmer, "Hochmittelalterliche Adelsfamilien", p. 12.

[87] *Notae Necrologicae Ebersbergenses*, pp. 77-78; for some reason, Ratold's daughter, Willibirg (I), is not so described although her death day is noted as that of her brother, Eberhard I, so the entry for her may be an incomplete afterthought (see 16 and 25 November). She is the only woman given any prominence in Williram's account and must have been a remarkable person. Many of these obits are also included in the Cartulary as recently noted by Wilhelm Störmer ("Hochmittelalterliche Adelsfamilien", p. 12, fn. 17).

[88] R. Le Jan, "L'épouse du comte due IXe au XIe siècle", pp. 24-28; this important issue is briefly noted for Bavaria in A. Schmid, "Comes und comitatus im süddeutschen Raum während des Hochmittelalters", pp. 203-04, who sets a significantly later date from the 12th century for its introduction.

to his estate at Persenbeug – granted Ebersberg castle itself with appurtenances to his wife Rihlint.[89] Unfortunately, we know nothing about Cotini other than her name which is the same as that of the older daughter of Tassilo, last Agilolfing duke of Bavaria, deposed by his cousin Charlemagne in 788/94.[90] It is difficult to know how much significance to assign to this one isolated piece of information; still, we must keep in mind that some of the family's later prominence and relationships may have derived from her and from the other wives of the counts, whether "countesses" or not.

For Sigihard, himself, we have a variety of evidence independent of Williram which allows us to understand the sources of his authority and his status with greater precision. In the first place, it is necessary to emphasize that there is no evidence that Sigihard ever exercised the normal judicial duties of a 9th century Bavarian *comes* or "sheriff".[91] Erwin Kupfer's study shows that several *comites* were active in the areas near Sempt and Ebersberg in the early 9th century, but for none of them does any connection to Sigihard seem probable.[92] And when Sigihard received his grant at Sempt ["ad Pergon"] from Arnolf in 888 it was described as "in comitatu Orendilonis" while the later grant in 896 at nearby Kaging was "in comitatu Regingarii".[93] Orendil and Regingar were the established royal *comites* or "sheriffs" responsible for the jurisdictions where these properties lay, and they would have presided in their courts over any disputes regarding them. Thus, it does not appear that Sigihard based his authority on the usurpation of any royal powers normally invested in the comital office over a Carolingian *comitatus* understood as a royally-authorized territorial jurisdiction.

In his meticulous study of comital authority and personnel in Carolingian Alemannia, Michael Borgolte argued that there were, in fact, two early forms of the comital office there. In "outer" Alemannia to the left of the Rhine, the jurisdictions were organized by *comitatus* separately from the royal fisc while in "inner" Alemannia to the right of the Rhine they were based directly upon fiscal estates.[94] Moreover, in "inner" Alemannia comital status could be derived directly from autogenous aristocratic power rather than by royal delegation. There is no evidence that Sigihard enjoyed any particular personal prominence in western Bavaria before his sudden documentary appearance in 888. Rather, it is probable that Sigihard's status derived from his delegated authority over fiscal properties beginning under King Karlmann when he was placed in charge of the royal marketplace at Sempt with the attendant properties and powers.[95] From Sempt there were several nearby opportunities to extend his authority, since the areas both immediately to the north and the south were particularly rich in fiscal estates.[96] The largest prize was, of course, the great royal forest to the south of Sempt; Sigihard's fortification at Ebersberg effectively annexed this substantial tract and opened the way for further acquisitions to the south.[97] Such an aggressive usurpation of regalian properties and powers would only have been possible during Arnolf's troubled final years and the weak rule of his son, Ludwig the Child. Thus, Sigihard's rise began

---

[89] *Cartular Ebersberg*, Nr I/35: "dedit coniugi sue Rihlindi castrum Eberespergense".

[90] See the comment in G. Mayr, *Ebersberg*, p. 104.

[91] It is difficult, therefore, to agree with L. Holzfurtner's assertion that, "ihr [the Ebersbergers'] Machtgefüge noch auf dem alten karolingischen Grafschaftssystem basiert hatte" ("Ebersberg – Dießen – Scheyern. Zur Entwicklung der oberbayerischen Grafschaft in der Salierzeit", in *Die Salier und das Reich*, vol. 1, ed. S. Weinfurter [Sigmaringen, 1991], pp. 549-77, here: p. 554); quite the opposite!

[92] E. Kupfer, "Karolingische Grafschaftsstrukturen", Map, p. 15. The evidence for this area is all assembled and discussed by Gottfried Mayr in S. Herleth-Krentz, *Erding*, pp. 18-22; and G. Mayr, *Ebersberg*, pp. 48-52.

[93] MGH, Diplomata, Arnolf, Nrs 5, 144.

[94] M. Borgolte, *Grafschaften Alemanniens*, pp. 248-57; according to Borgolte, these forms were combined under Louis the Pious.

[95] Sempt was located on the "salt road" from Reichenhall as was Föhring further along on the east bank of the River Isar. These marketplaces where salt served as the basic commodity, were located in both western and eastern Bavaria on fiscal properties under comital control as revealed by the royal inquest, the *Inquisitio de Theloneis Raffelstettensis*, held in 903x6 at Raffelstetten on the Danube regarding customary tolls (MGH, Capitularia regum Francorum, vol. 2, Nr 253, pp. 249-52). These early "para-urban" Bavarian marketplaces are examined above in Part I.3.

[96] Discussed thoroughly by Gottfried Mayr in S. Herleth-Krentz, *Erding*, pp. 15-18; and G. Mayr, *Ebersberg*, pp. 45-48.

[97] The best account of the early history of the Ebersberg forest is by Gottfried Mayr in his *Ebersberg*, pp. 243-45, who thinks the forest may have been attached to the fiscal estate at Sempt and, thus, granted to Sigihard in 888 which is possible. As Gottfried Mayr points out, the monastery later enjoyed regalian rights in the forest (see *Cartular Ebersberg*, Nrs I/2, 43,44), but these may have been the fruits of Sigihard's usurpation. Certainly, the establishment of Ebersberg secured Sigihard's <u>effective</u> control, whatever may have been the juridical status.

with loyal service to Karlmann at a time when that royal son's prospects were still in some doubt, and Sigihard's apparent kinship with Arnolf undoubtedly assisted his acquisition of additional properties as the surviving charter evidence clearly demonstrates. But Sigihard himself evidently brought about the decisive turn in his fortunes at the expense of his royal kinsmen and patrons.

Sigihard also enjoyed the benefits of kinship if he exercised some authority on behalf of Arnolf's mother, Liutswind, as was argued above with regard to the abbey of Moosburg. Indeed, such stewardships were a recognized means by which early-medieval aristocrats extended their influence and subordinated ecclesiastical property to their private uses.[98] However, there is no evidence that close connections to important churches and monasteries played a significant role in Sigihard's career.[99] He controlled a royal chapel at Sempt, but it was never transformed into an important cult site. Nor, so far as we know, was he an important patron of any monastery or, aside from the possible stewardship at Moosburg, did he (apparently) exercise any particular authority over ecclesiastical estates. From this perspective, Sigihard's career was remarkably "secular" although he was not adverse to the appropriation of spiritual charters for his worldly advantage. As we have seen, he was merely yielding to the urgent prophecies of holy men when he and his nephew erected the first fort at Ebersberg.

The early status of this site is worth some attention. Gottfried Mayr has argued that Ebersberg, in contrast to the older and nearby Egglburg, was a fortification of "the modern sort [*Typ*]", since it served the ongoing exercise of lordship [*Herrenburg*] rather than merely as a temporary place of refuge in troubled times [*Fliehburg*].[100] This places Sigihard's bold initiative at Ebersberg within the contemporary context of "encastellation" which subordinated the European countryside to various aristocratic lords rather than to royal authority.[101] While, as just indicated, I have no doubt that Sigihard was staking a claim to expanded lordship when he put up the first fortifications at Ebersberg, nevertheless, we must also realize that this was only the beginning of a process that was amplified and solidified by his heirs. Sigihard's fortifications were quite extensive as we should expect for a site intended for secure refuge, but even Abbot Williram's stirring tale indicates clearly that the first fort was a primitive stockade built entirely of wood.[102]

Although Sigihard's son and successor, Ratold, improved the fortifications and expanded the site at Ebersberg, it was evidently only under Ratold's son, Eberhard (I), that the fort ceased to be primarily a place of refuge. After a catastrophic fire which devastated the original site, Eberhard evidently rebuilt the fortifications hastily with a masonry wall, and he further improved the surrounding ditch or trench.[103] Thus, it was only now from the early 930s that Ebersberg would have appeared as something like a conventional castle defended by towers and provided with its own armory and workshops.[104] Williram describes Eberhard surveying the construction together with the "knights and ministerials" of his entourage (*cum multiudine militum ac ministrorum suorum*)". This was his retinue composed of both

---

[98] J-P. Poly and E. Bournazel, *The Feudal Transformation*, pp. 34-35.
[99] So also L. Holzfurtner, "Ebersberg – Dießen – Scheyern. Zur Entwicklung der oberbayerischen Grafschaft in der Salierzeit", p. 553.
[100] G. Mayr, *Ebersberg*, p. 100.
[101] J-P. Poly and E. Bournazel, *The Feudal Transformation*, pp. 25-28.
[102] This is evidently the earliest stratum identified during the necessarily limited excavations in 1978 and 1979 although the excavator, Walter Sage, is inclined to date these remains somewhat earlier in the 9th century than implied by Abbot Williram – but, if so, by whom and to what purpose? The excavation results and discussion are now published in W. Sage, "Klostergeschichte, die im Boden steckt – Ergebnisse der Ausgrabungen in der ehemaligen Grafenburg zu Ebersberg", p. 64. Unfortunately, I have not been able to review the other contributions to this volume which is unobtainable in North America; I thank Professor Wilhelm Störmer for drawing it to my attention (see his review in the *Zeitschrift für Bayerische Landesgeschichte).*
[103] *Chronicon Eberspergense*, pp. 10-11: "castrum muro circumdare, fossas ampliare caepit ... operariis suis demonstrare quales turres et officinas unoquoque loco construe vellet ...". This first masonary wall subsequently collapsed due to poor construction; W. Sage, "Klostergeschichte", pp. 64-67; whether the fire was a result of attack (so Sage) or accident remains unclear to me.
[104] Presumably, the "officinas" refer in the first place, following Classical usage, to facilities for arms-making, particularly a smithy, but the term might include other productive outbuildings and even storehouses. There is a useful, recent survey of Bavarian castle typology by C. Bachmann ("Funktion, Typologie und Geschichte früher Adelsburgen in Altbayern") which concentrates on the 11th and 12th centuries but also provides a short *excursus* outlining earlier developments which are still only known from isolated excavations (pp. 737-38).

free knights and unfree ministerials to whom he had undoubtedly distributed lands for their support and who can be traced through witness lists of benefactions recorded in the Ebersberg cartulary.[105] But we also learn from Abbot Williram that Ebersberg still was not garrisoned on a permanent basis nor was it provided with a suitable dwelling for extended residence by its lord and his family. That seems to have changed after Eberhard's divine vision although we may doubt that any of the family lived primarily at Ebersberg except in times of trouble.[106]

Nevertheless, Sigihard's descendants now possessed a place capable of serving as a center for family identity. And the final step for securing this dynastic status was also undertaken by Eberhard whose most important contribution, in Williram's eyes, was to erect the first church at Ebersberg. This was, according to Williram, an impressive stone structure measuring 80 feet in length and 50 in width, which finally completed the "civilization" of the site.[107] There Eberhard established a small college of canons secular, not a monastery of monks living independently under a rule, so that it remained completely under his control as a proprietary church, and he began to set aside property in 934, "for the redemption of the bodies and souls of his family and the well-being of his kinsmen and of all his successors".[108] The church and its priests thus served the family exclusively as a private chapel and chantry. Perhaps, it is this pronounced lack of ecclesiastical independence – that is, ongoing family control over all property and Hunfrid's compromised position as household chaplain – that explains why the episcopal ordinary, the bishop of Freising, was reluctant to consecrate the place.[109] Only after Eberhard's death and burial at Freising, did Ebersberg's ordinary finally grant license to his metropolitan (and Eberhard's kinsman), the archbishop of Salzburg in 970.[110] This at last allowed the church to become the site of the family's mausoleum only a generation before the final extinction of the dynasty.

In sum, Sigihard certainly established a lordship in western Old Bavaria incorporating regalian rights and properties which, to some degree, was autonomous from royal authority and readily capable of further expansion by his heirs. But, if we look, rather, for the "tokens of authority" that one normally associates with the "feudal transformation" – particularly feudal retinue, castle, cult center, and mythic "charter", all of which established dynastic identity – then I am inclined to designate Eberhard rather than Sigihard as the first "count" of Ebersberg. He seems to have had strong dynastic instincts; in 946 "our esteemed count Eberhard" successfully reclaimed by charter from Otto the Great property to the southeast in the Chiemgau which King Arnolf previously had granted in full ownership to "Sigihard, his grandfather".[111] Such explicit expressions of hereditary interests are exceedingly rare in royal charters and indicate a high degree of family consciousness. Moreover, Eberhard is the first member of the family for whom we have evidence that he exercised normal comital authority in a *comitatus* of his own in Old Bavaria, perhaps as early as 916 in the Donaugau and certainly by 950 in the area directly to the south of Ebersberg itself which was identified as being in Eberhard's *comitatus*.[112] It is true that

---

[105] As detailed in G. Flohrschütz, *Adel des Ebersberger Raumes*, *passim*.

[106] Abbot Williram informs us that at the time of the great battle at the River Lech in 955, Eberhard's sister, Willibirg, "tunc in sepe dicto castro morabatur". We know virtually nothing about other Ebersberger family residences although they must have maintained residences at a number of their rural estates which they could visit from time to time, as was the established custom of the early-medieval aristocracy, and possibly also a pied-à-terre in Regensburg for court business there.

[107] This first church has not been identified archaeologically; Sage is surely right to doubt the literal accuracy of Williram's account ("Klostergeschichte", p. 75, fn. 20).

[108] See *Cartular Ebersberg*, Nr I/1, p. 136: "pro redemptionem corporum animarumque suarum atque prosperitate parentum suorum et omnium successorum suorum".

[109] Bishops at this time varied widely in their attitudes and approaches to proprietary churches; see now S. Wood, *The Proprietary Church in the Medieval West*, pp. 812-24. Wood points out earlier (p. 368) that in comital disposition of properties pertaining to the endowment, "There is no reason to think the counts were being oppressive, as distinct from pursuing their own convenience ..."

[110] *Cartular Ebersberg*, Nr I/1, p. 136: "ipsum monasterium [sic] dedicatum est" (*cf.* p. 138, Nr 12). Williram, perhaps, out of embarrassment, ascribes the delay to the politics (see above, Part II.6).

[111] MGH, Diplomata, Otto I, Nr 78: "dilecto comiti nostro Eberhart nominato ... avo illius Sigihardo comiti ... in proprietatem donavit"; there is no surviving record of the original grant which was in the *comitatus* of the later *comes* Sigihard (see above), so the property may have been alienated by a cadet line after the first Sigihard's death.

[112] MGH, Diplomata, Konrad I, Nr 28 (916, i.e. before the death of his father, Ratold), for Bergheim on the north bank of the Donau 12 km west of Ingolstadt, "in comitatu Eberhardi in pago Tuonahgewe"; MGH, Diplomata, Otto I, Nr 126 (950), for a Neuching near (*in pago*) Öxing [= Grafing] "in comitatu Eberhardi comitis". It is not clear to me whether this "villa Neuching"

Sigihard was the object of divine prophecies which legitimated his usurpation at Ebersberg, but the clear continuity of this "foundation" episode with the later divine vision imparted to Eberhard raises the strong suspicion that the latter's chaplain, Hunfrid, was the first to formulate and propagate the entire family foundation myth in its extant form. Hunfrid's elaborate biblical exegesis, presented in laudatory detail by Abbot Williram's "Chronicle", clearly points to Hunfrid as the family's first ideologue, a role quite in keeping with his position as the long-serving clerical head of the family's chantry and, thus, its "memorial" custodian. The coherent combination of all of these "transformative" characteristics, marks Eberhard's comital lordship as clearly precocious.[113]

We can better understand the true nature of Sigihard's position by a comparison with his late 9th century contemporary, the Alsacian Eberhard whom we met in our exploration of Sigihard's origins (above, Part II.5). Although this earlier Eberhard seems to have enjoyed Arnolf's favor, he evidently lacked Sigihard's "Königsnähe"; nevertheless he clearly exercised greater authority over a richer territory quite removed from direct royal intervention. He was established at an ancient and still important "civitas", Strassburg, where he could exploit long established official authority with the support of the bishop, and Eberhard's personal comital authority also reached across the Rhine to the Ortenau in Alemannia. In addition to Gregorienthal, Eberhard controlled the southern Alsacian monastery of Lure (Lüders) through its stewardship to which he – like Sigihard at Moosburg? – succeeded as a kinsman of the royal mistress Waldrada. There his son, Hugo, lived "like a lord in his castle"; and Hugo was followed, in turn, by his son, Guntram.[114] Thus, for three generations Eberhard's family effectively appropriated the resources of this important foundation for their personal use. Eberhard was truly a "most illustrious count". Sigihard's backwoods trading post on the Sempt and his wooden stockade at Ebersberg seem quite primitive and provincial in comparison. The "feudal transformation" had not yet reached Bavaria in the late ninth century and was still only inchoate in the tenth.[115]

II.8 Epilogue:

Abbot Williram provides us with two interesting reflections on the comital office of the Ebersbergers. Both of them are attributed as a kind of a political testament to Count Ulrich who died in 1029. The first emphasizes royal authority and is presented as an exhortation to his sons on the occasion of their mother, Rihgart's funeral at Ebersberg in 1013, the very first family interment held at the church. There he charges them: "Never be rebellious to the king, nor in any way challenge the royal house, for then you will be despoiled of all your wealth."[116] The Ebersbergers had remained loyal to the Ottonian kings against the Bavarian duke and had survived, even prospered despite strong pressures. The occasion for Ulrich's second exhortation was a later gathering with his dependents, his "familiaribus", at Ebersberg castle. At the altar of St Sebastian in the church there Ulrich, now an aged widower, provides a melancholy reflection on current conditions which he attributes to neglect of the law. He then elaborates his indictment of the present age with a short history of the law which recalls the "Prologue" to the

---

is the old fiscal estate located about 8 kilometers north of Sempt and, thus, on the opposite side of the great forest from Öxing indicating a fairly extensive *comitatus* encompassing all of Sigihard's core possessions, but we should be wary of constructing an anachronistic Carolingian "Grafschaft Öxing-Steinhöring" as does L. Holzfurtner ("Ebersberg – Dießen – Scheyern", p. 554); see now also G. Diepolder, "Bischof Abraham von Freising und achtzehn Grafen", p. 282, who identifies Neuching with the fiscal estate. In the following year, 951, another charter refers, as G. Diepolder argues (*loc. cit.*), to a property at Itzling, about 13 km northeast of Erding "in comitatu Adelberonis", very likely Eberhard's brother, Adalbero I (MGH, Diplomata, Otto I, Nr 126). Thus, in the mid-10th century the two brothers had broad comital authority over this ancient landscape east and south of the Isar.

[113] So S. Wood, *Proprietary Church*, p. 365, sees, "A men's monastery or collegiate church, often of modest size and built in or beside a castle, belonging outright to a noble family, recording the family's history, perhaps inventing its genealogy, and serving for several generations as its burial-place and focal point, is more characteristic of the eleventh and twelfth centuries than of the ninth or tenth ..."

[114] See the short account in H. Hummer, *Politics and Power*, pp. 224-26, based upon the "Life" of St Deicolus (AASS 2, 18 January), Cap. 7: "ac si miles castrensis, invictus existeret" (Hummer's translation).

[115] For the later development of comital institutions in high-medieval Bavaria, see now the overview in A. Schmid, "Comes und Comitatus".

[116] *Chronicon Eperspergense*, p. 14: "Regi numquam rebelletis, vel domum ulla occasione vocetis, quia tunc opes vestri disperdentur."

Bavarian Law Code.[117] In his youth – so Ulrich reminisces – it was considered shameful to be illiterate just as it had been in the time of Charlemagne, and he and his contemporaries had applied themselves to study of the law. Now, all was different, contemporaries neglected to teach their sons the law, and as a result, justice was perverted.[118]

As in other early historical sources, it is hardly likely that these are verbatim transcripts of actual speeches. Still, we may suspect that Abbot Williram was ascribing thoughts to Ulrich which were at least a credible reflection of family philosophy. After all, the "Chronicle" was being written within 50 years of Ulrich's death at a time when persons who had known him probably were still alive. Ulrich had lived under the royal (and imperial) regime of Heinrich II (r. 1002/1014-1024), former duke of Bavaria (r. 994x5-1004) and son of Duke Heinrich the Quarrelsome who had convened the assembly at Ranshofen.[119] Ulrich himself had probably attended Ranshofen with the other *comites* and may well have been convinced of the necessity for the "Constitutions" enacted there. They represented the political course of the future which the younger Heinrich was to pursue as king and emperor. Their evocation of the older Carolingian legal order was evidently congenial to Ulrich who clearly saw Charlemagne as a model ruler.[120] But at the end of the childless Heinrich's reign or during the early years of his Salian successor, Konrad II (r. 1024/1027-1039) – just when Ulrich was addressing his *familiaribus* at St. Sebastian's altar – this self-conscious "Renovatio Regni Francorum" (so Heinrich's seal) was, in Ulrich's view, endangered.

If Ulrich's high view of the *comes* as a royal official truly represents the family's view of their office, then the "counts" of Ebersberg – despite their imposing positions – were still very much like the "sheriffs" of Carolingian Bavaria, and the "feudal transformation" was still quite incomplete in Bavaria. Fortunately, we have an extremely rare and vivid witness to the legal responsibilities of his son, Adalpero II, during Ulrich's last years and under the new Salian regime. In the summer of 1027 Emperor Konrad II was returning from Italy where on 26 March he had just received the imperial title in Rome from Pope John XIX. By early July he was in Regensburg where, as was customary at the beginning of a reign, he took the oaths of all the Bavarian *comites* and others authorized to determine legal matters (*electos iudices*), and, by their sworn evidence, Konrad conducted an inquest into all Bavarian properties to determine the extent of imperial possessions there.[121] During this process a "certain *comes* Poppo" declared that the abbey of Moosburg was free and not subordinate (*servire*) to the episcopal church of Freising, "unless this can be refuted within its own comital jurisdiction and in public court (*in mallo publico*) by sworn jurors (*scabinis*)."[122] Thus, Poppo, who is otherwise unknown in Bavaria, asserted that Moosburg pertained to the emperor's authority.[123] Now, it will be remembered that in 908 Sigihard had been party to a suit which ostensibly resolved this issue in Freising's favor (above, Part II.5), and the bishop of Freising, Egilbert, immediately raised objections to this renewed attempt at alienation of a valuable monastic foundation. In the event, Konrad, after considering the matter, then directed Adalpero, "in whose *comitatus* that same place Moosburg is located" to hold an inquest at his court "according to Bavarian law" (*in placito suo ... iuxta legem Baioaricam*) and determine the truth of the matter.

---

[117] *Chronicon Eperspergense*, p. 14: "Cum Romani terrarum orbi imperarent, ita moderamine legum scripto regebatur, ut nulli impune cederet factum, quod lex vetuerat. Postquam vero Germanum regnum a Romanis recesserat, Sigipertus et Theodericus ac deinde Carolus iura dictabant…" The Merovingian kings Theuderich, Childebert, Chlothar and Dagobert are all mentioned as legislators in the "Prologue" of the Bavarian Law Code (*Lex Bav*) but not a Sigibert of whom there were three Merovingians by that name. Nor does any of the surviving manuscript variants have a "Sigibert" so this may be a clerical slip for one of the better known "-berts".

[118] See the comments by P. Johanek, "Zur rechtlichen Funktion von Traditionsnotiz, Traditionsbuch und früher Siegelurkunde", pp. 147-48.

[119] See above, Part II.3.

[120] This differs sharply from the reading of S. Weinfurter, "Zentralisierung", p. 289. The Carolingian connection is emphasized by illustrated genealogical diagrams on facing pages at the beginning of the volume containing the "Chronicle" and the "Cartulary" where the Carolingian dynasty and the Ebersbergers are presented in parallel, probably as an evocation of Sigihard's documented kinship (described by P. Johanek, "Zur rechtlichen Funktion", pp. 149-50).

[121] *Trad. Freising*, Nr 1422, pt. 2, p. 278: "ubi [Regensburg] inter cetera que ad imperii sui statum utilitatemque pertinere videbantur placuit omnes Baioarice provintie comites et electos iudices per sacramentum regale admonere ut possessiones et predia infra eandem provintiam sita que novissent ad solium sui imperii iure pertinere eodem sacramento publice interrogati manifest pronutiarent."

[122] *Trad. Freising*, Nr 1422, pt. 2, p. 278: "nisi hoc in comitatu et in mallo publico a veridicis contradiceretur scabinis."

[123] He does not occur elsewhere in the Freising deeds, but he was in the imperial entourage in May 1027 at Verona as second of the 8 *comites* who were present at a judgment against Duke Adalbero of Carinthia (MGH, Diplomata, Konrad II, Nr 92).

On 8 August Adalpero promptly and duly assembled "a public and lawful session of court" (*placitum suum publice legitimeque*) at Tittenkofen, an estate between the rivers Sempt and Strogen about 13 kilometers south of Moosburg.[124] There he presided with four other *comites* including Poppo and Adalpero's own brother, Eberhard. Clearly, this dispute was treated with great urgency and care – just as the emperor had directed. At this court, after arguments had been made both by the bishop's and the emperor's legal advocates and evidence presented, all the jurors (*iudices omnes*) numbering more than 21 including two other *comites* awarded Moosburg to Freising, and the bishop took possession "on customary comital authority" (*banno consueto ... banno comitis*). Of course, we do not know whether this was a conclusion actually desired by the emperor for Freising's benefit but which could not be authorized without the requisite legalities: in other words, a legal charade. We only know that, on the face of it, Adalpero presided over legal proceedings which, through their strict adherence to the law, diminished the imperial interest. Thus, there arose a potentially disastrous conflict between obedience and justice, both of which – so his father Count Ulrich had urged – must be observed.

Did the aged Ulrich, who placed such emphasis on obedience to the Crown, approve of Adalpero's apparent concern for legality over imperial favor?[125] Freising certainly viewed Adelpero favorably and clearly considered him as well as his father to be a friend of the bishopric. In a slightly later deed of exchange from 1034 between Bishop Egilbert and Adalpero, the *comes* is fulsomely celebrated as, "the son of the most vigorous Count Ulrich, governing according to the rule of comital justice in the Norican province".[126] Amongst the repetitive *formulae* of the property exchanges which dominate the documentary record from the later 9th century, the record of the dispute over Moosburg provides an exceptional insight into the functioning of a Bavarian court, albeit under exceptional circumstances. But there may be more to its purpose. This Freising deed of 1027 in its circumstantial and enthusiastic legal details echoes the records of court sessions two centuries earlier under the Carolingians, and a certain predisposition to legal antiquarianism may also be present. Poppo's by now somewhat archaic Frankish term "mallum/s publicum/s" instead of "placitum" for a royal court reappears here in the Freising records for the first time since 804; similarly "scabinus" was last seen in 825.[127] Presumably, this idiosyncratic usage identifies Poppo as a non-Bavarian, an outsider, but it also suggests that Adalpero and his colleagues were acting exactly like their Carolingian predecessors as royal *missi* even though this term is never used. The careful elaboration of the legal record certainly reflects the importance of the case for Freising, but it also may be constructed to emphasize a characteristic of Adelpero's family, their fastidious concern for legal tradition, which subsequently informed Abbot Williram's account in the Ebersberg record. We do not know whether a similar legal scrupulosity characterized other comital dynasties.

---

[124] Tittenkofen was located at the northern edge of the Ebersberger's central lordship but does not seem to have been one of their properties.

[125] Or, perhaps, Abbot Williram unwittingly presented Adalpero's own thoughts on the law. His father, Ulrich's praise of the law to his retainers contains puzzling references to his lack of "nepotes", and the subsequent prophecy by the hermit, Gunther, of his imminent death and the division of his wealth amongst those other than his cognates raises the question of whether there is some confusion of the *obiter dicta* here attributed to Ulrich with the circumstances of his son Adalpero II, the last male of the line, who died in 1045 far away from Ebersberg at the family estate of Persenbeug on the Danube.

[126] *Trad. Freising*, Nr 1438a, pt. 2, p. 292: "cum Adalperone filio Odalrici strenuissimi comitis regula iustitiae Norice comitatum provintiae gubernante". The purpose of the exchange was to secure properties which Adelpero granted to Ebersberg. The awkward and virtually untranslatable encomium of Adelpero's comital authority in the Freising record is absent from Ebersberg's copy of the deed (b).

[127] *Trad. Freising*, Nrs 193b (p. 183), 195 (p. 186), 514 (p. 438: *scabini constituti*); these term are otherwise extremely rare in Bavaria. There is another isolated, contemporary and apparently unrelated instance of the term "in public mallo" in *Trad. Freising*, Nr 1441a,b.

Bibliography of Works Cited

A. Primary Sources

All of the Monumenta Germaniae Historica (MGH) texts cited here are now freely available from a database maintained by the Bavarian State Library (Bayerische Staatsbibliothek), Munich, which can be accessed on-line over the dMGH link at www.mgh.de.

Annales Regni Francorum et Annales qui dicuntur Einhardi, ed. F. Kurze, MGH, Scriptores Rerum Germanicarum in Usum Scholarum [vol. 6], (1895); English translation: *Carolingian Chronicles*, transl. B. Scholz and B. Rogers (Ann Arbor, 1970).

Cartular Ebersberg: Das Cartular des Klosters Ebersberg, ed. F. Graf Hundt, Abhandlungen der historischen Classe der königlichen bayerischen Akademie der Wissenschaften, vol.14/3 (Munich, 1879), pp. 115-96.

Chronicon Eberspergense, ed. W. Arndt, MGH, Scriptores, vol. 20 (1868), pp. 9-15.

Codex Diplomaticus Fuldensis, ed. E. Dronke (1850).

Dokumente zur Geschichte von Staat und Gesellschaft in Bayern, vol. 1/1, Altbayern bis 1180, ed. K.-L. Ay (Munich, 1974)

Ex Chronico Eberspergensi Posteriore, ed. G. Waitz, MGH, Scriptores, vol. 25 (1880), pp. 867-72.

Leges Baiuwariorum, ed. J. Merkel, MGH, Leges (in Folio), vol. 3 (1863), pp. 484-85.

Lex Bav: *Lex Baiwariorum*, ed. E. von Schwind, MGH, Leges Nationum Germanicarum, vol. 5/2 (1926); English translation: *Laws of the Alamans and Bavarians*, transl. T. Rivers (Philadelphia, 1977).

MGH, Capitularia regum Francorum, vol. 1, ed. A. Boretius (1883).

MGH, Capitularia regum Francorum, vol. 2, ed. A. Boretius and V. Krause (1890-97).

MGH, Diplomata, Arnolf: Die Urkunden Arnolfs, ed. P. Kehr, MGH, Die Urkunden der deutschen Karolinger, vol. 3 (1940).

MGH, Diplomata, Friedrich I: Die Urkunden Friedrichs I., ed. H. Appelt *et al.*, Die Urkunden der deutschen Könige und Kaiser, vols. 10/1, 10/3 (1975, 1985).

MGH, Diplomata, Karl III: Die Urkunden Karls III., ed. P. Kehr, Die Urkunden der deutschen Karolinger, vol. 2 (1936-37).

MGH, Diplomata, Konrad I: Die Urkunden Konrad I, Heinrich I. und Otto I, Die Urkunden der deutschen Könige und Kaiser, vol. 1, ed. T. Sickel (1879-84).

MGH, Diplomata, Konrad II: Die Urkunden Konrads II., ed. H. Bresslau, Die Urkunden der deutschen Könige und Kaiser, vol. 4 (1909).

MGH, Diplomata, Ludwig the Child: Die Urkunden Zwentibolds und Ludwgs des Kindes, ed. T. Schieffer, Die Urkunden der deutschen Karolinger, vol. 4 (1960).

MGH, Diplomata, Ludwig the German: Die Urkunden Ludwigs des Deutschen, Karlmanns und Ludwigs des Jüngeren, ed. P. Kehr, Die Urkunden der deutschen Karolinger, vol. 1 (1932-34).

MGH, Diplomata, Otto I: Die Urkunden Konrad I, Heinrich I. und Otto I., ed. T. Sickel, Die Urkunden der deutschen Könige und Kaiser, vol. 1 (1879-84).

MGH, Diplomata, Otto II: Die Urkunden Otto des II., ed. T. Sickel, Die Urkunden der deutschen Könige und Kaiser, vol. 2/1 (1888).

MGH, Diplomata, Otto III: Die Urkunden Otto des III., ed. T. Sickel, Die Urkunden der deutschen Könige und Kaiser, vol. 2/2 (1893).

Notae Necrologicae Ebersbergenses, ed. F. Baumann, MGH, Necrologia Germaniae, vol. 3 (1905), pp. 77-78.

Notitia Arnonis und *Breves Notitiae*. Die Salzburger Güterverzeichnisse aus der Zeit um 800: Sprachlich-historische Einleitung, Text und Übersetzung", ed. F. Losek, in Mitteilungen der Gesellschaft für Salzburger Landeskunde, vol. 130 (1990), pp. 5-192.

Trad. Freising: *Die Traditionen des Hochstifts Freising*, 2 parts, ed. T. Bitterauf, Quellen und Erörterungen zur bayerischen und deutschen Geschichte, New Series, vols. 4,5 (Munich, 1905; reprint: Aalen, 1967): all page references are to part 1 unless otherwise noted.

Trad. Passau: *Die Traditionen des Hochstifts Passau*, ed. M. Heuwieser, Quellen und Erörterungen zur bayerischen und deutschen Geschichte, New Series, vol. 6 (Munich, 1930; reprint: Aalen, 1988).

Trad. Regensburg: *Die Traditionen des Hochstifts Regensburg und des Klosters S. Emmeram*, ed. J. Widemann, Quellen und Erörterungen zur bayerischen und deutschen Geschichte, New Series, vol. 8 (Munich, 1943; reprint: Aalen, 1988).

Trad. Weissenburg: *Traditiones Wizenburgenses. Die Urkunden des Klosters Weissenburg, 661-864*, ed. A. Doll and K. Glöckner, Arbeiten der hessischen historischen Kommission Darmstadt (Darmstadt, 1979).

Das Verbrüderungsbuch der Abtei Reichenau, ed, J. Autenrieth *et al.*, MGH, Libri Memoriales et Necrologia, Nova Series, vol. 1 (1979).

Vita Karoli: Einhardi Vita Karoli Magni, ed. O. Holder-Egger, MGH, Scriptores Rerum Germanicarum in Usum Scholarum [vol. 25] (1911); English translation: *Two Lives of Charlemagne*, ed. and transl. D. Ganz (London, 2008).

Vita Severini: Eugippius, Das Leben des Heiligen Severin. Lateinisch und Deutsch, ed. R. Noll (Passau, 1981).

B. Secondary Sources

Die Abendländische Freiheit vom 10. zum 14. Jahrhundert, ed. J. Fried, Vorträge und Forschungen, vol. 39 (Sigmaringen, 1991).

Adam, H., *Das Zollwesen im fränkischen Reich und das spätkarolingische Wirtschaftsleben*, Beiheft der Vierteljahrschirft für Sozial- und Wirtschaftsgeschichte, Nr 126 (Stuttgart, 1996).

Alföldy, G., *Noricum* (London & Boston, 1974).

Babucke, V., "Die Ausgrabungen 'Hinter dem Schwalbeneck 5-9' in Augsburg", *Das Archäologische Jahr in Bayern 2000*, pp. 84-91.

Bachmann, C., "Funktion, Typologie und Geschichte früher Adelsburgen in Altbayern", in *Hochmittelalterliche Adelsfamilien*, pp. 729-48.

Banzhaf, M., *Unterschichten in bayerischen Quellen des 8. bis 11. Jahrhunderts*, Materialien zur bayerischen Landesgeschichte, vol. 9 (Munich, 1991).

Barrington Atlas of the Greek and Roman World, ed. R. Talbert (Princeton, 2000).

Barthélemy, D., *The Serf, the Knight and the Historian*, rev. Engl. edn (Ithaca & London, 2009).

Bayerischer Geschichtsatlas, ed. M. Spindler and G. Diepolder (Munich, 1969).

Bayerisches Städtebuch, ed. E. Keyser and H. Stoob, Deutsches Städtebuch, vol. 5 in 2 Parts (Stuttgart et al., 1971/74).

Becher, M., *Eid und Herrschaft. Untersuchungen zum Herrscherethos Karls des Großen*, Vorträge und Forschungen, Sonderband 39 (Sigmaringen, 1993).

Bischoff, B., *Die süddeutschen Schreibschulen und Bibliotheken in der Karolingerzeit*, Part 1: Die bayerischen Diözesen, 3rd edn (Wiesbaden, 1974).

Bisson, T., *The Crisis of the Twelfth Century; Power, Lordship, and the Origins of European Government* (Princeton & Oxford, 2009).

Boos, A., et al., "Regensburg zwischen Antike und Mittelalter", in *Regensburg im Mittelalter*, pp. 31-44.

Borgolte, M., *Die Grafen Alemanniens in merowingischer und karolingischer Zeit. Eine Prosopographie*, Archäologie und Geschichte, vol. 2 (Sigmaringen, 1986).

idem, "Die Geschichte der Grafengewalt im Elsaß von Dagobert I. bis Otto dem Großen", *Zeitschrift für die Geschichte des Oberrheins*, vol. 131 (1983), pp. 3-54.

idem, *Geschichte der Grafschaften Alemanniens in fränkischer Zeit*, Vorträge und Forschungen, Sonderband 31 (Sigmaringen, 1984).

Bosl, K., *Die Sozialstruktur der mittelalterlichen Residenz- und Fernhandelsstadt Regensburg. Die entwicklung ihres Bürgertums vom 9.–14. Jahrhundert*, Abhandlungen der bayerischen Akademie der Wissenschaften, Phil.-hist. Kl., N.F. Nr 63 (Munich, 1966).

Bowlus, C., *The Battle of Lechfeld and its Aftermath, August 955: the End of the Age of Migrations in the Latin West* (Aldershot & Burlington, VT, 2006).

Brandl-Ziegert, R., "Die Sozialstruktur der bayerischen Bischofs- und Residenzstädte Passau, Freising, Landshut und Ingolstadt", in *Die Mittelalterliche Stadt in Bayern*, ed. K. Bosl, Beihefte der Zeitschrift für bayerische Landesgeschichte, Reihe B/6 (Munich, 1974), pp. 18-127.

Brown, W., *Unjust Seizure; Conflict, Interest and Authority in an Early Medieval Society* (Ithaca & London, 2001).

Brühl, C., *Palatium und Civitas. Studien zur Profantopographie spätantiker Civitates vom 3. bis zum 13. Jahrhundert*, vol. 2 (Cologne & Vienna, 1990).

Bühler, H., "Die Herkunft des Hauses Dillingen", in *Die Grafen von Kyburg*, Schweizer Beiträge zur Kulturgeschichte und Archäologie des Mittelalters (Olten & Freiburg i.B., 1981), pp. 9-30.

The Cambridge Urban History of Britain, vol. 1, ed. D. M. Palliser (Cambridge, 2000).

Christlein, R., "Die rätischen Städte Severins", in *Severin zwischen Römerzeit und Völkerwanderung* (Linz, 1982), pp. 217-53

Campbell, J., *The Anglo-Saxon State* (London & New York, 2000).

Czysz, W., "Das zivile Leben in der Provinz", in *Die Römer in Bayern*, pp. 177-308.

Davis, J., "A Pattern for Power: Charlemagne's Delegation of Judicial Responsibilities", in *The Long Morning of Medieval Europe; New Directions in Early Medieval Studies*, ed. J. Davis and M. McCormick (Aldershot & Burlington, VT, 2008), pp. 235-46.

Deutinger, R., *Königsherrschaft im Ostfränkischen Reich. Eine pragmatische Verfassungsgeschichte der späten Karolingerzeit*, Beiträge zur Geschichte und Quellenkunde des Mittelalters, vol. 20 (Ostfildern, 2006).

Diepolder, G., "Bischof Abraham von Freising und achtzehn Grafen", *Zeitschrift für Bayerische Landesgeschichte*, vol. 68 (2005), pp. 275-88.

Diestelkamp, B., "Freiheit der Bürger – Freiheit der Stadt", in *Die Abendländische Freiheit*, pp. 485-510.

Dietz, K., and T. Fischer, *Die Römer in Regensburg* (Regensburg, 1996).

Dollinger, P., *Der bayerische Bauernstand vom 9. bis zum 13. Jahrhundert*, German edn and transl. F. and U. Irsigler (Munich, 1982).

Geschichte Salzburgs. Stadt und Land, vol. 1/2, ed. H. Dopsch (Salzburg, 1983).

Emmerig, H., "Die Münz und Geldgeschichte der Stadt Regensburg", in *Regensburg im Mittelalter*, pp. 159-76, with maps.

Endemann, T., *Markturkunde und Markt in Frankreich und Burgund vom 9. bis 11. Jahrhundert* (Konstanz & Stuttgart, 1964).

Ennen, E., "Different Types of Formation of European Towns", English translation in *Early Medieval Society*, ed. S. Thrupp (New York, 1967), pp. 174-182; reprinted from *Le Moyen Âge*, vol. 62, in her *Gesammelte Abhandlungen zum europäischen Städtewesen und zur rheinischen Geschichte*, ed. G. Droege *et al*. (Bonn, 1977), pp. 134-42.

The Erosion of History; Archaeology and Planning in Towns, ed. C. Heighway, Council for British Archaeology – Urban Research Committee (1972).

Fehn, K., *Die zentralörtliche Funktionen früher Zentren in Altbayern* (Wiesbaden, 1970).

Fichtenau, H., *Das Karolingische Imperium. Soziale und geistige Problematik eines Großreiches* (Zürich, 1949).

Fischer, K., "Im Namen Gottes und des Geschäfts zur Stadtfreiheit – Fernhändlertum und Autonomie der Kommune Regensburg im Mittelalter", in *Regensburg im Mittelalter*, pp. 147-58.

Flohrschütz, G., *Der Adel des Ebersberger Raumes im Hochmittelalter*, Schriftenreihe zur bayerischen Landesgeschichte, vol. 88 (Munich, 1989).

Fried, J., "The Frankish Kingdoms, 817-911: The East and Middle Kingdoms", in *The New Cambridge Medieval History*, vol. 2, pp. 142-68.

Der frühmittelalterliche Staat – europäische Perspektiven, ed. W. Pohl and V. Wieser, Forschungen zur Geschichte des Mittelalters, vol. 16 (Vienna, 2009).

Ganshof, F., *Was ist das Lehnswesen?*, 6th German ed. (Darmstadt, 1983).

Gieysztor, A., "Les marches et les merchandises entre le Danube et la Volga aux viiie-xie siècles", in *Mercati e Mercanti nell'Alto Medioevo: L'Area Euroasiastica e l'Area Mediterranea*, Settimane di Studio del Centro Italiano di Studi sull'Alto Medioevo, vol. 40 (Spoleto, 1993), pp. 499-518.

Glaser, F., *Frühes Christentum im Alpenraum. Eine archäologische Entdeckungsreise* (Regensburg, 1997).

Goldberger, P., "Cities, Place and Cyberspace", University of California, Berkeley, 1 February 2001 (www.paulgoldberger.com/speeches).

Goodhart, M., "Sovereignty: Reckoning What is Real", *Polity*, vol. 34 (2001), pp. 241-57.

Gutmann, F., *Die soziale Gliederung der Bayern zur Zeit des Volksrechtes*, Abhandlungen aus dem Staatswissenschaftlichen Seminar zu Strassburg i. E., vol. 20 (Strassburg, 1906).

Guttenberg, E. von, "Iudex h.e.comes aut grafio. Ein Beitrag zum Problem der fränkischen 'Grafschaftsverfassung' in der Merowingerzeit", in *Festschrift Edmund E. Stengel*, ed. E. Kunz (Münster & Cologne, 1952), pp. 93-129.

Hammer, C., "'Crowding the King': Rebellion and Political Violence in late-Carolingian Bavaria and Italy", *Studi Medievali*, 3rd Ser., vol. 48 (2007), pp. 493-541.

idem, "Early Merovingian Bavaria: A Late-Antique Italian Perspective", *Journal of Late Antiquity* (2011, forthcoming).

idem, "'The Examples of the Saints': Reading Eugippius' Account of Saint Severin", *Classica et Mediaevalia*, vol. 59 (2008), pp. 155-85.

idem, "For All the Saints; Bishop Vivolo and the Origins of the Feast", *Revue Mabillon*, n.s. vol. 15 (2004), pp. 5-26.

idem, *From Ducatus to Regnum; Ruling Bavaria under the Merovingians and Early Carolingians*, Collection Haut Moyen Âge, vol. 2 (Turnhout, 2007).

idem, "The handmaid's tale: morganatic relationships in early-medieval Bavaria", *Continuity and Change*, vol. 10 (1995), pp. 345-68.

idem, "Hoc and Hnaef in Bavaria? Early-Medieval Prosopography and Heroic Poetry", *Medieval Prosopography*, vol. 26 (2009 for 2005), pp. 13-50.

idem, *A Large-Scale Slave Society of the Early Middle Ages; Slaves and their Families in early medieval Bavaria* (Aldershot & Burlington, VT, 2002).

idem, "Land Sales in eighth- and ninth-century Bavaria: legal, economic and social Aspects", *Early Medieval Europe*, vol. l6 (1997), pp. 47-76.

idem, "*Lex scripta* in early medieval Bavaria: use and abuse of the *lex baiuvariorum*", in *Law in Medieval Life and Thought*, ed. E. King and S. Ridyard, Sewanee Medieval Studies, Nr 5 (Sewanee, 1990), pp. 185-95.

idem, "*Pipinus Rex*: Pippin's Plot of 792 and Bavaria", *Traditio*, vol. 63 (2008), pp. 235-76.

idem, "The Social Landscape of the Prague Sacramentary; The Prosopography of an Eighth-Century Mass-Book", *Traditio*, vol. 54 (1999), pp. 41-80.

Handbuch der bayerischen Geschichte, vol. 1, ed. M. Spindler, 2nd edn (Munich, 1981).

Handbuch der bayerischen Kirchengeschichte, vol. 1/1, ed. W. Brandmüller (St Ottilien, 1998).

Handbuch der Historischen Stätten, Bayern I, ed. H.-M. Körner and A. Schmid (Stuttgart, 2006).

Hannig, J., "Zur Funktion der karolingische 'missi dominici' in Bayern und in den südöstlichen Grenzgebieten", *Zeitschrift der Savigny Stiftung für Rechtsgeschichte, Germanistische Abteilung*, vol. 101 (1984), pp. 256-300.

Hardt-Friedrichs, F., "Markt, Münze und Zoll im ostfränkischen Reich bis zum Ende der Ottonen", *Blätter für deutsche Landesgeschichte*, vol. 116 (1980), pp. 1-31.

Herleth-Krentz, S., and G. Mayr, *Das Landgericht Erding*, Historischer Atlas von Bayern, Teil Altbayern, vol. 58 (Munich, 1997).

Hlawitschka, E., *Vom Frankenreich zur Formierung der europäischen Staaten- und Völkergemeinschaft 840-1046*, (Darmstadt, 1986).

Hochmittelalterliche Adelsfamilien in Altbayern, Franken und Schwaben, ed. F. Kramer and W.

Störmer, Studien zur bayerischen Verfassungs- und Sozialgeschichte, vol. 20 (Munich, 2005).

Hodges, R., *Dark Age Economics; The origins of towns and trade A.D. 600-1000* (London & New York, 1982).

Hodges, R., *Towns and Trade in the Age of Charlemagne* (London, 2000).

Holzfurtner, L., "Ebersberg – Dießen – Scheyern. Zur Entwicklung der oberbayerischen Grafschaft in der Salierzeit", in *Die Salier und das Reich*, vol. 1, ed. S. Weinfurter (Sigmaringen, 1991), pp. 549-77.

idem, "*Pagus Huosi* und Huosigau. Untersuchungen zur Gaulandscaft im westlichen Oberbayern", in *Land und Reich, Stamm und Nation. Festschrift für Max Spindler zum 90. Geburtstag*, vol. 1, ed. A. Kraus, Schriften zur bayerischen Landesgeschichte, vol. 78 (Munich, 1984), pp. 287-304.

Hummer, H., *Politics and Power in Early Medieval Europe; Alsace and the Frankish Realm, 600-1000* (Cambridge, 2005).

Innes, M., *State and Society in the Early Middle Ages; The Middle Rhine valley, 400-1000* (Cambridge, 2000).

Jahn, J., *Ducatus Baiuvariorum. Das Bairische Herzogtum der Agilolfinger*, Monographien zur Geschichte des Mittelalters, vol. 35 (Stuttgart, 1991).

Johanek, P., "Die Raffelstetter Zollordnung und das Urkundenwesen der Karolingerzeit", in *Festschrift für Berent Schwineköper zu seinem siebszigsten Geburtstag*, ed. H. Maurer and H. Patze (Sigmaringen, 1982), pp. 87-103.

idem, "Zur rechtlichen Funktion von Traditionsnotiz, Traditionsbuch und früher Siegelurkunde", in *Recht und Schrift im Mittelalter*, ed. P. Classen, Vorträge und Forschungen, vol. 23 (Sigmaringen, 1977), pp. 131-62.

Keller, H., *Kloster Einsiedeln im Ottonischen Schwaben*, Forschungen zur Oberrheinischen Landesgeschichte, vol. 13 (Freiburg i.B., 1964).

Kienast, W., *Die fränkische Vasallität. Von den Hausmeiern bis zu Ludwig dem Kind und Karl dem Einfältigen*, Frankfurter Wissenschaftliche Beiträge, Kulturwissenschaftliche Reihe, vol. 18 (Franfurt, 1990).

Kobler, G., "*Civitas* und *vicus, burg, stat, dorf* und *wik*", in *Vor- und Frühformen*, pp. 61-76.

Kohl, T., *Lokale Gesellschaften. Formen der Gemeinschaft in Bayern vom 8. Bis zum 10. Jahrhundert*, Mittelalter-Forschungen, vol. 29 (Ostfildern, 2010).

Kottje, R., "Die Lex Baiuvariorum – Das Recht der Bayern", in Überlieferung und Geltung normativer Texte des frühen und hohen Mittelalters, ed. H. Mordek, Quellen und Forschungen zum Recht im Mittelalter, vol. 4 (Sigmaringen, 1986), pp. 9-23.

Krah, A., *Absetzungsverfahren als Spiegelbild von Königsmacht*, Untersuchungen zur deutschen staats- und Rechtsgeschichte, N.F., vol. 26 (Aalen, 1987).

eadem, "Die fränkisch-karolingische Vasallität seit der Eingliederung Bayerns in das Karolingerreich", *Zeitschrift für Bayerische Landesgeschichte*, vol. 56 (1993), pp. 613-30.

Kupfer, E., "Karolingische Grafschaftsstrukturen im bayrisch-österreichischen Raum", *Mitteilungen des Instituts für Österreichische Geschichtsforschung*, vol. 111 (2003), pp. 1-17.

Le Jan, R., "L'épouse du comte due IXe au XIe siècle: Transformation d'un modèle et idéologie du pouvoir", in her *Femmes, pouvoir et société dans le haut Moyen Age* (Paris, 2001), pp. 21-29.

Loré, F., "Wohnraum statt Gräber – Cannabae legionis in Regensburg größer als erwartet', in *Das Archäologische Jahr in Bayern 2008*, pp. 96-98.

Maddicott, J. R., "London and Droitwich, *c.* 650-750: trade, industry and the rise of Mercia", *Anglo-Saxon England*, vol. 34 (2005), pp. 7-58.

Mayr, G., *Ebersberg, Gericht Schwaben*, Historischer Atlas von Bayern, Teil Altbayern, vol. 48 (Munich, 1989).

idem, "Die Grafen von Kühbach und ihr Verwandtschaftskreis", in *Hochmittelalterliche Adelsfamilien*, pp. 97-139.

McCormick, M., "New Light on the Dark Ages; How the Slave Trade Fuelled the Carolingian Economy", *Past and Present*, Nr 177 (2002), pp. 17-54.

Mitterauer, M., "Jahrmarktkontinuität und Stadtentstehung", abbreviated version in *Annales, É.S.C.*, vol. 28, now complete in his *Markt und Stadt im Mittelalter*, pp. 154-91.

idem, *Karolingische Markgrafen im Südosten. Fränkische Reichsaristokratie und bayerischer Stammesadel im österreichischen Raum*, Archiv für österreichische Geschichte, vol. 123 (Vienna, 1963).

idem, *Markt und Stadt im Mittelalter. Beiträge zur historischen Zentralitätsforschung*, Monographien zur Geschichte des Mittelalters, vol. 21 (Stuttgart, 1980).

idem, "Wirtschaft und Verfassung in der Zollordnung von Raffelstetten", reprinted from *Mitteilungen des Oberösterreichischen Landesarchivs*, vol. 8, in his *Markt und Stadt im Mittelalter*, pp. 235-65.

idem, *Warum Europa? Mittelalterliche Grundlagen eines Sonderweges* (Munich, 2003); English translation: *Why Europe? Medieval Origins of its Special Path* (Chicago, 2010).

Müller-Mertens, E., "The Ottonians as Kings and Emperors", in *The New Cambridge Medieval History*, vol. 3, pp. 233-66.

München, Bayern und das Reich im 12. und 13. Jahrhundert, ed. H. Seibert and A. Schmid, Beihefte zur Zeitschrift für bayerische Landesgeschichte, vol. 29 (Munich, 2008).

The New Cambridge Medieval History, vol. 2, ed. R. McKitterick (Cambridge, 1995).

The New Cambridge Medieval History, vol. 3, ed. T. Reuter (Cambridge, 1999).

Pohl, W., "Staat und Herrschaft im Frühmittelalter: Überlegungen zum Forschungsstand", in *Staat im frühen Mittelalter*, pp. 9-38.

Poly, J.-P., and E. Bournazel, *La mutation féodale X^e –XIIe siècle*, Nouvelle Clio, vol. 16 (Paris, 1980); English translation: *The Feudal Transformation 900 – 1200* (New York & London, 1991).

Prinz, F., "Herzog und Adel im agilulfingischen Bayern", reprinted from *Zeitschrift für bayerische Landesgeschichte*, vol. 25 (1962), pp. 283-311, with a "Nachtrag 1964" in *Zur Geschichte der Bayern*, ed. K. Bosl, Wege der Forschung, vol. 60 (Darmstadt, 1965), pp. 225-63.

idem, "Die innere Entwicklung: Staat, Gesellschaft, Kirche, Wirtschaft", in *Handbuch der bayerischen Geschichte*, pp. 350-518.

Regensburg im Mittelalter, vol. 1: Beiträge zur Stadtgeschichte vom frühen Mittelalter bis zum Beginn der Neuzeit, ed. M. Angerer *et al.* (Regensburg, 1995).

Reichsstädte in Franken. Katalog zur Ausstellung, ed. R. Müller *et al.*, Veröffentlichungen zur Bayerischen Geschichte und Kultur, vol. 14/87 (Munich, 1987).

Reinecke, P., "Turum, Iovisura, Patrensibus, Sorviodurum, Augustis", reprinted in his *Kleine Schriften zur Vor- und Frühgeschichtlichen Topographie Bayerns* (Kallmünz, 1962), pp. 49-65.

Reindel, K., "Die politische Entwicklung", in *Handbuch der bayerischen Geschichte*, pp. 249-349.

Reuter, T., "Debate: The 'Feudal Revolution' III", Past & Present, Nr 155 (1997), pp. 177-95.

idem, *Germany in the early middle ages, c. 800-1056* (London & New York, 1991).

Reynolds, S., "The Writing of medieval urban history in England", reprinted in her *Ideas and Solidarities of the Medieval Laity* (Aldershot, 1995), Nr XV.

Die Römer in Bayern, ed. W. Czysz *et al.* (Stuttgart, 1995).

Sage, W., "Klostergeschichte, die im Boden steckt – Ergebnisse der Ausgrabungen in der ehemaligen Grafenburg zu Ebersberg", in *Kloster Ebersberg. Prägekraft christlich – abendländischer Kultur im Herzen Altbayerns*, ed. B. Schäfer (Ebersberg, 2002), pp. 53-76.

Schieffer, R., "Die internationale Forschung zur Staatlichkeit in der Karolingerzeit", in *Der frühmittelalterliche Staat*, pp. 43-49.

Schlesinger, W., "Der Markt als Frühform der deutschen Stadt", in *Vor- und Frühformen*, pp. 262-93.

Schmid, A., "Comes und comitatus im süddeutschen Raum während des Hochmittelalters", in *Regensburg, Bayern und Europa. Festschrift für Kurt Reindel zum 70. Geburtstag*, ed. L. Kolmer and P. Segl (Regensburg, 1995), pp. 189-212.

Schmid, P., "Die Herrschaftsträger und ihre Einflußsphären im früh- und hochmittelalterlichen Regensburg", in *Regensburg im Mittelalter*, pp. 45-56.

Schnurbein, S. von, "Die kulturgeschichtliche Stellung des nördlichen Rätien", *Bericht der Römisch-Germanischen Kommission*, vol. 63 (1982), pp. 5-16.

Schulz, K., "Von der familia zur Stadtgemeinde. Zum Prozeß der Erlangung bürgerlicher Freiheitsrechte durch hofrechtlich gebundene Bevölkerungsgruppen", in *Die Abendländische Freiheit*, pp. 461-84.

Schwarz, K., *Archäologisch- Topographische Studien zur Geschichte frühmittelalterlicher Fernwege und Ackerfluren im Alpenvorland zwischen Isar, Inn und Chiemsee*, Bayerisches Landesamt für Denkmalpflege, Abteilung Bodendenkmalpflege, vol. 45/1 (Kallmünz, 1989).

Severin zwischen Römerzeit und Völkerwanderung (Linz, 1982).

Staat im frühen Mittelalter, ed. S. Airlie, W. Pohl and H. Reimitz, Forschungen zur Geschichte des Mittelalters, vol. 11 (Vienna, 2006).

Stoclet, A., *Immunes ab Omni Teloneo. Étude de diplomatique, de philologie et d'histoire sur l'exemption de tonlieux au haut Moyen Age et spécialement sur la 'Praeceptio de navibus'*, Institut Historique Belge Rome Bibliothèque, vol. 45 (Brussels & Rome, 1999).

Störmer, W., *Adelsgruppen im früh- und hochmittelalterlichen Bayern*, Studien zur bayerischen Verfassungs- und Sozialgeschichte, vol. 4 (Munich, 1972).

idem, "Augsburg zwischen Antike und Mittelalter. Überlegungen zur Frage eines herzoglichen Zentralortes im 6. Jahrhundert und eines vorbonifatianischen Bistums", in *Adel und Königtum im mittelalterlichen Schwaben: Festschrift für Thomas Zotz zum 65. Geburtstag*, ed. A. Bihrer *et al.*, Veröffentlichungen der Kommission für Geschichtliche Landeskunde in Baden-Württemberg, vol. B 175 (Stuttgart, 2009), pp. 71-85.

idem, *Früher Adel. Studien zur politischen Führungsschicht im fränkisch- deutschen Reich vom 8. bis 11. Jahrhundert*, Monographien zur Geschichte des Mittelalters, vol. 6, 2 Parts (Stuttgart, 1975).

idem, "Hochmittelalterliche Adelsfamilien: Probleme, vor die uns die Quellen Stellen", in *Hochmittelalterliche Adelsfamilien*, pp. 9-38.

idem, Review of W. Sage, "Klostergeschichte", in the *Zeitschrift für Bayerische Landesgeschichte*, vol. 66 (2003), pp. 640-42.

idem, "Zur politische Bedeutung und zur topographischen Lage der Pfalz Karls des Großen in Regensburg", *Mitteilungen des Instituts für österreichische Geschichtsforschung*, vol. 117 (2009), pp. 1-11.

Strayer, J., *On the Medieval Origins of the Modern State* (Princeton, 1970).

Studien und Vorarbeiten zur Geschichte des grossfränkischen Adels, ed. G. Tellenbach, Forschungen zur oberrheinischen Landesgeschichte, vol. 4 (Freiburg/Breisgau, 1957).

Sturm, J., *Die Anfänge des Hauses Preysing*, Schriftenreihe zur bayerischen Landesgeschichte, vol. 8 (Munich, 1931; reprint: Aalen, 1974).

Ubl, H., "Die archäologische Erforschung der Severinsorte und das Ende der Römerzeit im Donau-Alpen Raum" in *Severin zwischen Römerzeit und Völkerwanderung*, pp. 71-97.

Ulbert, G., "Zur Grenze zwischen den römischen Provinzen Norikum und Raetien am Inn", *Bayerische Vorgeschichtsblätter*, vol. 36 (1971), pp. 101-23.

Vollmer, F., "Die Etichonen. Ein Beitrag zur Kontinuität früher Adelsfamilien", in *Studien und Vorarbeiten*, pp. 137-84.

Vor- und Frühformen der europäischen Stadt im Mittelalter, ed. H. Jankuhn *et al.*, Part 1, Abhandlungen der Akademie der Wissenschaften in Göttingen, Phil.-hist. Kl., 3. Folge, Nr 83 (Göttingen, 1973).

Wanderwitz, H., *Studien zum mittelalterlichen Salzwesen in Bayern*, Schriftenreihe zur bayerischen Landesgeschichte, vol. 73 (Munich, 1984).

Weinfurter, S., "Die Zentralisierung der Herrschaftsgewalt im Reich durch Kaiser Heinrich II", *Historisches Jahrbuch*, vol. 106 (1986), pp. 241-97.

Weitlauff, M., "Bischof Ulrich von Augsburg (923-973). Leben und Wirken eines Reichbischofs der ottonischen Zeit", in *Bischof Ulrich von Augsburg 890-973*, ed. M. Weitlauff, Jahrbuch des Vereins für Augsburger Bistumsgeschichte e.V., vol. 26/27 (Weißenhorn i.B., 1993), pp. 69-142.

Wickham, C., *Framing the Early Middle Ages; Europe and the Mediterranean 400-800* (Oxford, 2005).

idem, *The Inheritance of Rome; A History of Europe from 400 to 1000* (London, 2009)

Wolfram, H., "Bavaria in the Tenth and Early Eleventh Centuries", in *The New Cambridge Medieval History*, vol. 3, pp. 293-309; German version with more extensive literature citations in his, *Salzburg, Bayern, Österreich*, pp. 380-98.

idem, *Die Geburt Mitteleuropas. Geschichte Österreichs vor seiner Entstehung* (Vienna & Berlin, 1987).

idem, *Salzburg, Bayern, Österreich. Die Conversio Bagoariorum et Carantanorum und die Quellen ihrer Zeit*, Mitteilungen des Instituts für Österreichische Geschichtsforschung, Ergänzungsband 31 (Vienna & Munich, 1995)

Wood, S., *The Properietary Church in the Medieval West* (Oxford, 2006).

Wormald, P., "Pre-modern 'State' and 'Nation': definite or indefinite?", in *Staat im frühen Mittelalter*, pp. 179-89.

Zöllner, E., "Rugier oder Russen in der Raffelstettener Zollurkunde?", *Mitteilungen des Instituts für Österreichische Geschichtsforschung*, vol. 60 (1952), pp. 108-19.

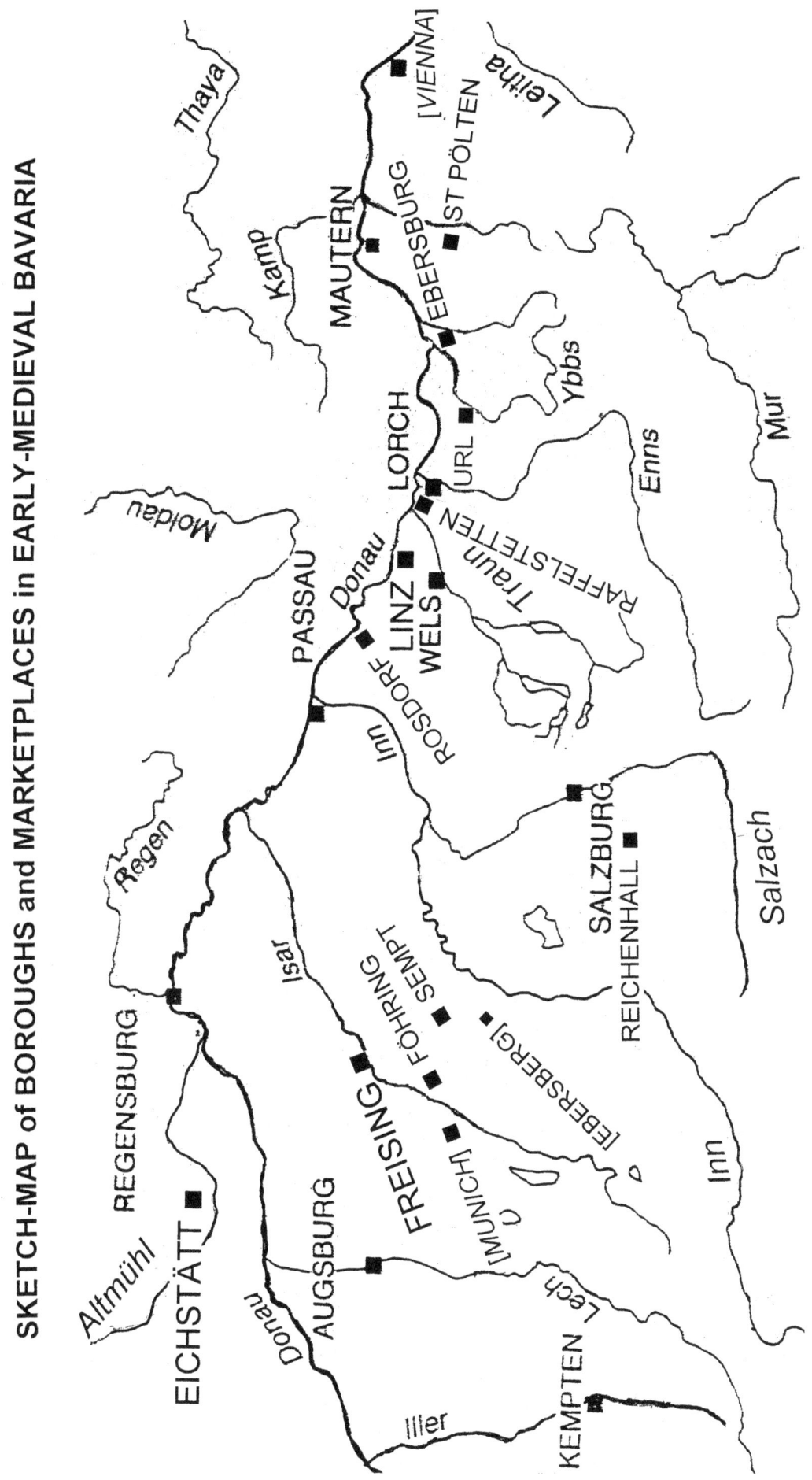

CITY PLAN of EARLY-MEDIEVAL REGENSBURG
(Source: C. Brühl, *Palatium und Civitas* 2)

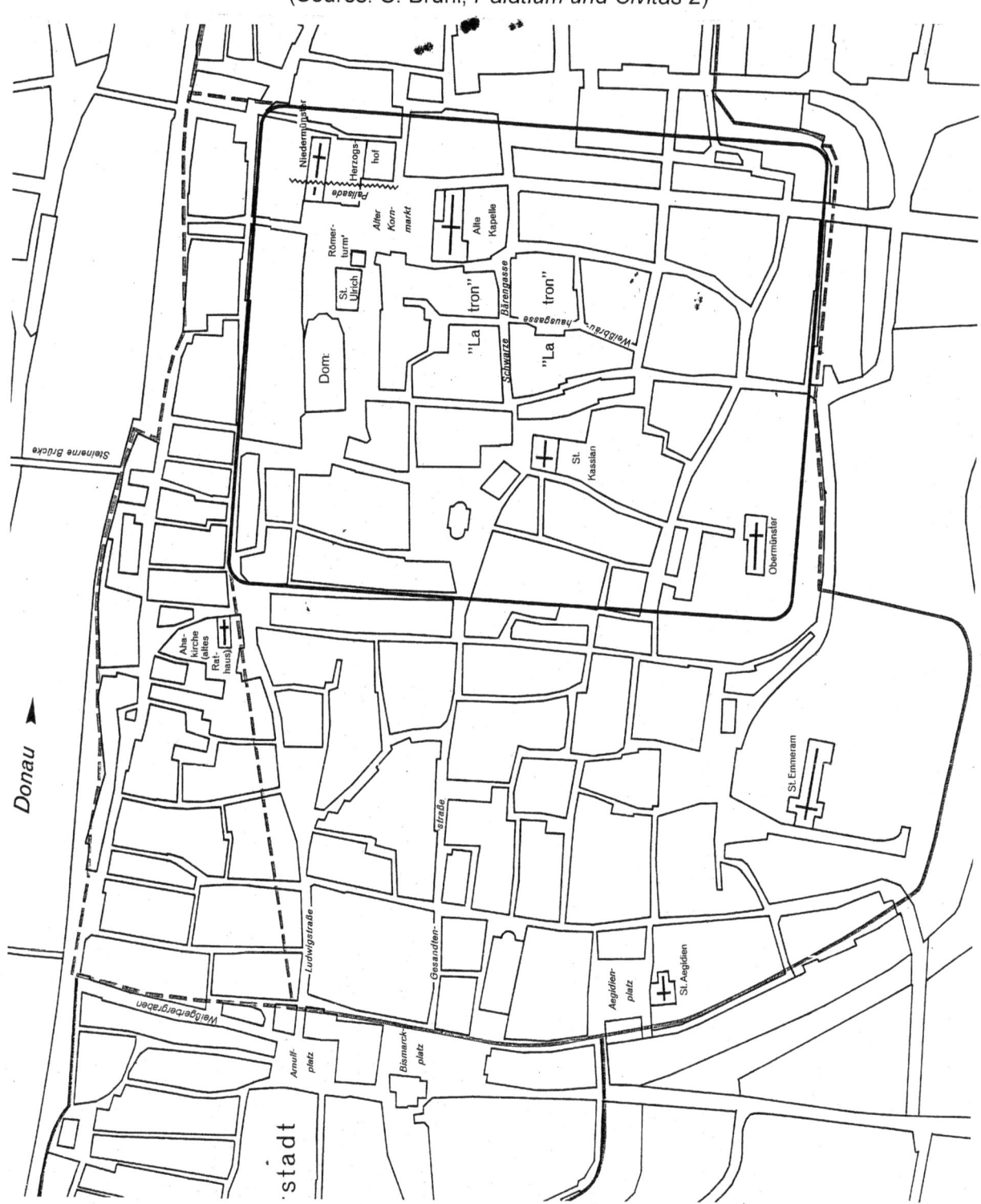

EXHIBIT I.1: PROTO-URBANISM in EARLY-MEDIEVAL BAVARIA before ca 1000

	REGENSBURG	PASSAU	SALZBURG	AUGSBURG	EICHSTÄTT	FREISING
ROMAN PREDECESSOR	LEGIONARY CASTRA with CANABAE	OPPIDUM	MUNICIPIUM	MUNICIPIUM (CAPITAL)	NIL	NIL
TRANSPORTATION ACCESS	DANUBE/ROMAN ROAD	DANUBE/ROMAN ROAD	SALZACH-INN/ROMAN ROAD	LECH/ROMAN ROAD	ALTMÜHL/FRANKISH ROAD	ISAR/ROMAN ROAD
FORTIFICATION	LEGIONARY CASTRA/"BURG"	CASTRUM/URBS	CASTRUM SUPERIUS/ "BURG"	RUINOUS ROMAN WALL REBUILT in 10th c/ "BURG"	URBS after 908	CASTRUM
DUCAL/ROYAL PALACE	ROYAL & DUCAL	DUCAL	DUCAL ROYAL?	?	NIL	DUCAL? ROYAL?
EARLY EPISCOPAL SEAT	X	X	METROPOLITAN after 798	X	X	X
MAJOR MONASTERY	St EMMERAM	NIEDERNBURG	St PETER /NONNBERG	St AFRA (PILGRIMMAGE)	St WALBURGA	St STEPHAN?
MARKET and TOLL	By early 10th c. ROYAL	EPISCOPAL (999)	By early 10th c. EPISCOPAL (996)	?	EPISCOPAL (908)	EPISCOPAL (996)
MINT	ROYAL MINT as REGIONAL STANDARD	EPISCOPAL [use of REGENSBURG STANDARD] (999)	EPISCOPAL [use of REGENSBURG STANDARD] (996)	?	EPISCOPAL [use of REGENSBURG STANDARD] (908)	EPISCOPAL [use of REGENSBURG STANDARD] (996)
FAIR	by 1030	?	?	by 1030	?	?
CIVIC ORGANIZATION	ROYAL by 880s with LOCAL OFFICIALS	EPISCOPAL by 976?	?	?	?	?
CIVIC TENEMENTS	by 893	by 976?	?	?	?	?

Exhibit I.2

Regensburg Cartulary Deed Nr 93 (880x885)

In the Name of the Supreme God. Be it known to all men of the Christian religion who desire to know such matters that I, Ratheri, considering forgiveness in the future and mindful of the obligation which I have taken upon myself, have conveyed to the altar of God which stands consecrated to the honor of the Holy Martyr, Emmeram, my own slavewoman, Ellinpurg, acquired by my own resources. And after my death I have appropriated my own estate to that place on this condition: that she might expect protection and guardianship there and pay nothing yearly beyond four pennies and also arrange the balance or her life according to her own judgment. Finally, I have released my three sons named Alawin, Johannes and Bernhard, whom the above named woman bore me, as freemen and safe from every bond of human servitude. With my brothers named Allin and Alawin present and consenting with willing mind in both matters, that is concerning the woman and the boys. This was done, moreover, in the presence of the citizens (*civibus*) of the Royal Borough (*urbis regie*) of Regensburg whose names appear below: Lantolt the Under-Deputy of the City (*subvicarius civitatis*), Adalpero the Toll Collector (*exactor telonei*), Odalman, Egilolf, Ratker, Wolffrid, Ratcoz, Huntolf, Otwin, Welo, Wachio, Adalrat, Enci.

Charter of King Arnulf Nr 116 (5 June 893)

... by request of Rihharii, our abbot (*custodis nostri*) ... we have granted to the abbey of Metten ... within the borough (*urbe*) of Regensburg five lots (*curtilia*) with all of the buildings pertaining there and directly next to the tenement (*curte*) which is called "Odalmann's hovesteti", adjacent and contiguous, which [lots] are seen to be between the intersection of two streets (*viarum*) which meet on the west side of the aforesaid tenement, that is Odalmann"s hovesteti" ...

Charter of Emperor Otto II Nr 137 (ca 976?)

In the name of the holy and individual Trinity, Otto, by the favor of God's grace, Emperor Augustus. Be it known to all of the holy Church of God and to our faithful retainers, both present and future, how our esteemed and faithful Piligrim, venerable bishop of the church of Passau, having related to us how the fidelity and good will of the people of Passau was an aid to our rule, proceeded to request and in every wise implore that they might receive some security of life and conduct from our imperial might, lest in the future they be taxed by any sort of exaction (*ullius exactionis censu constringantur*). And hearing these petitions of the aforesaid bishop with pious ears, we order that the tenants (*possessores*) of the aforewritten city (*civitatis*) henceforth not be made to pay any toll upon all the waters of our realm neither upstream nor downstream, nor by any means (? *nihilominus*) be constrained to render any quit-rent (*censum*) for the plots (*areis*) which they possess within the same city. And the family of St Mary (Niedermünster), both men and women, shall not be bound henceforth to any unjust distraint of service ...

Exhibit I.3

May the zeal of all the Christian faithful, both present and future, know that with regard to the clamor and complaint of all the Bavarians, viz. of the bishops, abbots and the sheriffs and of all others who journey into the eastern parts, how they came before King Ludwig [IV, "The Child", 900-11] maintaining that they were bound and compelled by unjust tolls (*theloneo*) and unfair travel levies (*muta*) in those parts. And he, hearing this with favorable disposition, according to the practice of the kings, his ancestors, enjoined the Margrave Arbio, together with those justices in the eastern regions to whom this becomes known, to look into the toll regulations and to investigate the rates of the tolls. And he assigned Archbishop Theotmar [of Salzburg], Bishop Burchard of Passau, and Sheriff Otachar as his commissioners in order that they might reform this rightly and justly in his stead. And these are those who gave evidence under oath concerning the tolls within the comital jurisdiction of Arbio: Waldo the Deputy, Durinc the Deputy [+ 39 other men including Eigil the Deputy]. These and all others who were noble men within these three shires, after swearing an oath, were questioned by the Margrave Arbio in the presence of Archbishop Theotmar and Bishop Burchard of Passau and Sheriff Otachar sitting at the plea sessions held at the place called Raffelstetten. And they returned the toll stations and the rates of the tolls as they were paid most justly in the times of Ludwig ["The German", 817/26-76] and Karlmann [876-80] and of other Kings.

1) Boats coming from western regions which, after they have passed out of the Forest of Passau, intend to land at Rosdorf or wherever and hold a market should render a semidragmam in toll, that is, one scot. If they intend to proceed further downstream to Linz, should render three half-measures, that is, three bushels of salt from each boat. With regard to slaves and other goods, they should pay nothing there. Rather, afterwards, they may have permission to land and to sell wherever they wish, right up to the Bohemian Forest.

2) If anyone from Bavaria wants to send his salt to his own residence, and this is attested on oath by the steersman of the boat, he should not pay anything. Rather, he may pass through quietly.

3) If, on the other hand, any freeman passes through a lawfully established market, neither paying nor declaring anything there, and he is convicted of it, let both the boat and the cargo be taken from him. Moreover, if someone's slave commits this, let him be detained there until his master comes and pays the indemnity, and, afterwards, he may depart.

4) If, moreover, Bavarians or those Slavs who live within this country should enter into that same region to buy provisions with slaves or horses or cattle or their other produce, let them buy whatever is needed without tolls wherever they wish within that region. Moreover, if they wish to pass through a market, let them pass right across the middle of the square without any hindrance. And let them buy without tolls in other places within the region as they are able. If they would prefer to trade at the market itself, let them pay the prescribed tolls and let them buy whatever they like, as much as they are able.

5) Moreover, carts from the saltworks which pass over the Enns on the public highway, should only pay one full bushel at the River Url and not be made to pay anything more. But the boats there which come from the Traungau District should pay nothing. Rather, they may pass through without any levy. All of this is to be observed with regard to Bavarians only.

6) On the other hand, Slavs coming from amongst the Rus and the Bohemians, in order to trade, wherever they may set up trading-posts, whether along the shores of the Danube or amongst the inhabitants living along the Rodl or in the Riedmark, let each be liable to pay two lumps of beeswax, each worth one scot, for each horse's packload. For a man's packload let him pay one lump of the same value. Moreover, if he intends to sell slaves or horses, let him pay one tremissis for a female slave and the same amount for a stallion, but one saiga for a male slave and the same for a mare. Bavarians, on the other hand, and those Slavs who live within this country should not be made to pay anything while buying and selling there.

7) Item, with regard to boats from the saltworks, after they have passed through the Bohemian Forest, they should not have permission either to buy, to sell or even to land at any place before they have reached the Ebersburg. There, for each boat of normal size, that is, one which is manned by a crew of three, they should pay three bushels of salt, and nothing more should be required of them. Rather, they may proceed on the Mautern or to wherever else a salt market might be established at that time, and there they should make a similar payment, that is, three bushels of salt, and nothing more. And afterwards, they should have free and secure permission to sell and to buy without any regulation by the sheriff (*banno comitis*) or restrictions from any other person. Rather, at whatever fair price (*meliori pretio*) the seller and the buyer agree between themselves to exchange their goods, they may have free and unrestricted permission to do so.

8) If, on the other hand, they intend to pass on through to the market of the Moravians, according to the assessment of the merchandise, let them pay one shilling for each boat at that time and let them pass through with permission. However, on return they should not be made to pay any rightful obligations.

9) Professional merchants, that is, Jews and all other professional merchants, wherever they may come from, whether from this country or from other countries, should pay the lawful tolls, both for slaves and for other goods, as was always the case under the kings in earlier times.

EXHIBIT I.4: BAVARIAN TRADE Along the DANUBE RIVER as DESCRIBED in the RAFFELSTETTEN INQUEST

SECTION and PLACES	PARTICIPANTS/TRANSPORT	COMMODITIES
1-4: Along the DANUBE RIVER from the FOREST of PASSAU to the BOHEMIAN FOREST		
TOLL STATION at ROSDORF MARKET	BOATS from the WEST	SALT SLAVES Other GOODS
MARKET at LINZ and beyond	FREE BAVARIANS and their SLAVES SUPPLYING their own RESIDENCES by BOAT	Their own SALT
	BAVARIANS or SLAVS from BAVARIA coming to BUY PROVISIONS	PURCHASE PROVISIONS SELL SLAVES, HORSES and CATTLE, or their other PRODUCTS
5-6: From the HIGHWAY CROSSING at the RIVER ENNS		
TOLL STATION at the RIVER URL	CARTS of BAVARIANS from the SALTWORKS	SALT
	BOATS of BAVARIANS from the TRAUN DISTRICT	SALT
Along the SHORES of DANUBE and with those living along the RODL and in the RIEDMARK	SLAVS COMING from the RUS and BOHEMIANS to TRADE	BEESWAX MALE and FEMALE SLAVES MARES and STALLIONS
	BAVARIANS and SLAVS from BAVARIA BUYING and SELLING THERE	
7-8: Beyond the BOHEMIAN FOREST		
TOLL STATION at EBERSBURG (YBBS)	BOATS from the SALTWORKS with STANDARD CREW of THREE	SALT
SALT MARKET at MAUTERN (KREMS) or ELSEWHERE		SALT
MARKET of the MORAVIANS		SALT MERCHANDISE
9: All MARKETS	JEWS and other PROFESSIONAL MERCHANTS from BAVARIA and ELSEWHERE	SLAVES UNSPECIFIED GOODS

Exhibit II.1

1. Freising Deed Nr 313, 15 January 814

In the Name of God. I, Sheriff Orendil, pondering and considering about my soul and the future life in order that I might be worthy to receive from a merciful Lord abundant forgiveness for my sins, convey to the Cathedral Church of St Mary, Ever Virgin, and of St Corbinian, Christ's Confessor, at Freising, my own acquired property in a place which is called Schammach for the redemption of my soul and of my kinsmen in this manner, that it be allowed me to hold it while I live. After my death no one should be able to gainsay that whatever I have in the same place remains to the Cathedral Church of St Mary. If, however, any of my sons might be so worthy that he should attain the office of Sheriff, I desire and establish this, that with the advice of the Bishop he may receive the aforesaid property in benefice on the condition that he render ten shillings in silver there from as rent to the Cathedral Church of St Mary. These are the witnesses tugged by the ears: [9 laymen + 4 clerks]. This was done on the 18th Calends of February, in the 14th year of the Most Glorious Emperor Karl Augustus, in the sixth Indiction. I Tagibert, unworthy deacon, wrote this little charter at the injunction of the Lord Bishop Hitto.

2. Law Code of the Bavarians, Title 2, 14-15

Courts should be held on the first day of the month, or even fortnightly if necessary, to inquire into offences so that there may be peace in the country. And all freemen shall assemble on the appointed days wherever the Justice shall ordain. And no one who dwells within the jurisdiction of the Sheriff shall dare refuse to come to the court; whether a vassal of the King or the Duke, all shall come to the court, and anyone who neglects to come shall be fined 15 shillings. Moreover, the Sheriff should have with him a Justice who is authorized to render judgment there and also a law-book, so that they may always render a right judgment. With regard to any offence which requires compensation, let him who offended against the law pay compensation as the law requires, and let him hand over a pledge to the Sheriff as "peace-money" as the law provides.

The Justice also should receive his share from any case that he judges ... From every amount paid in compensation he should always receive the third part so long as he judges rightly.

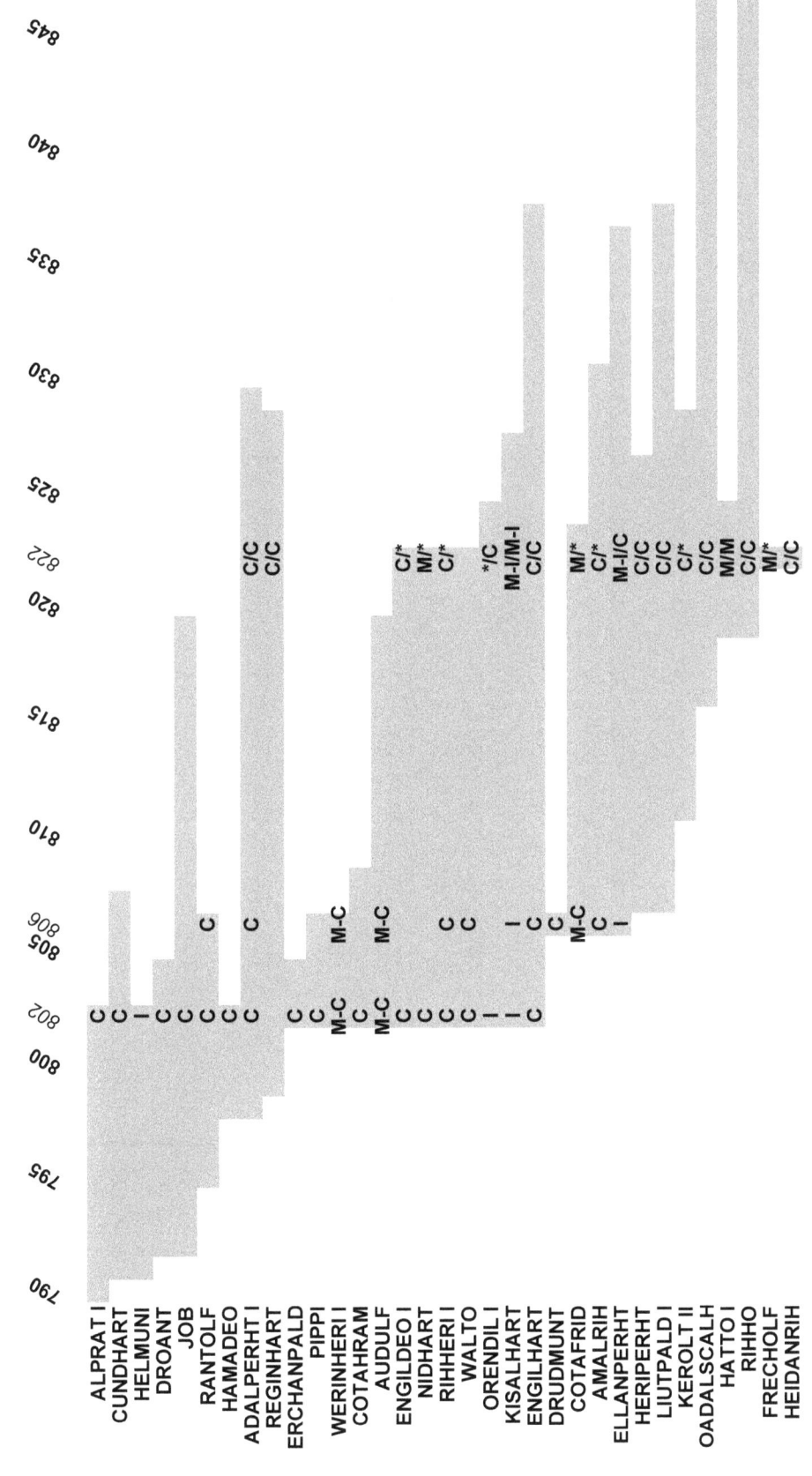

EXHIBIT II.2: DATED OFFICIAL SPANS for SENIOR LAYMEN ATTENDING BAVARIAN MISSATICAL COURTS

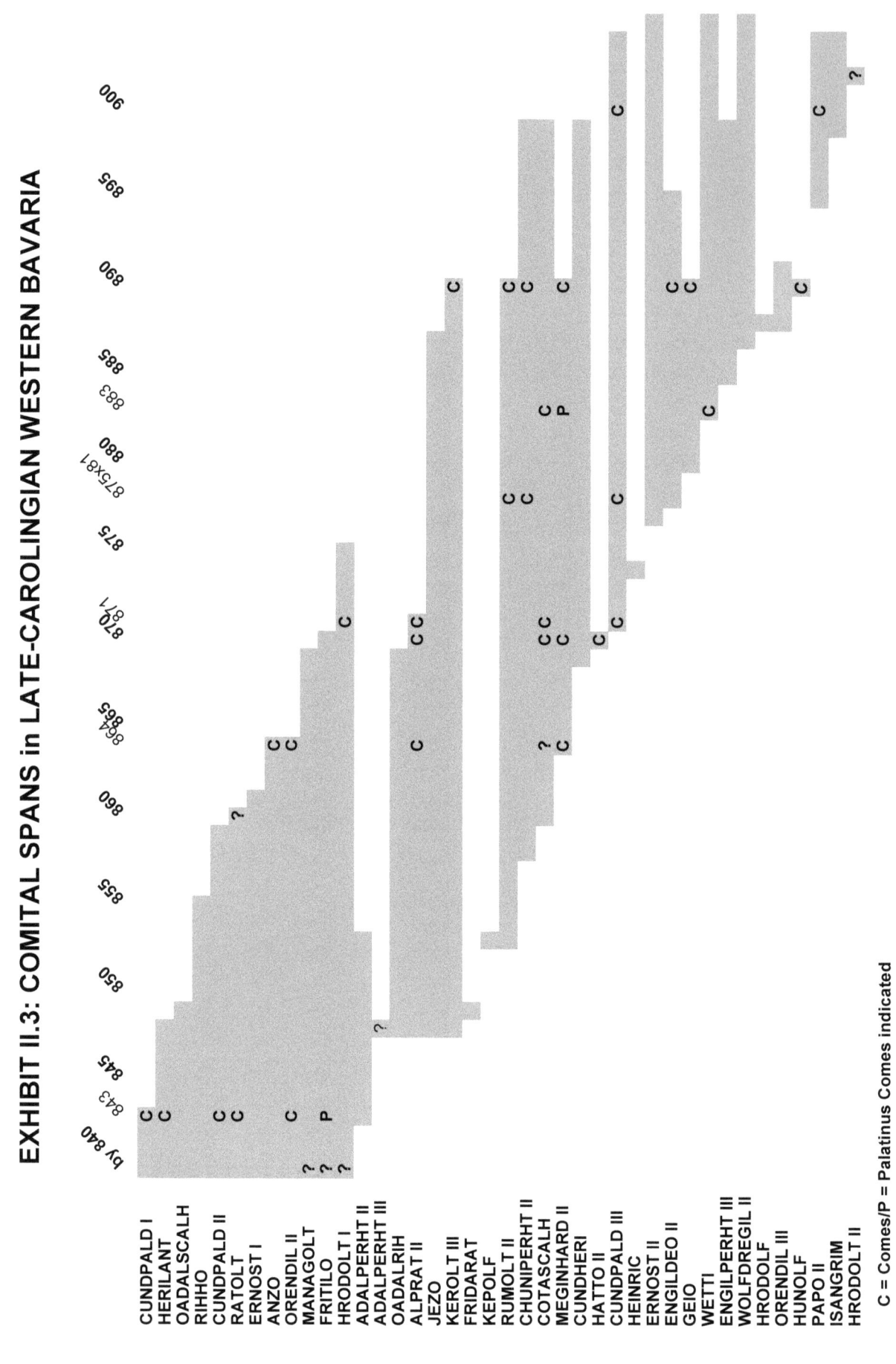

Exhibit II.4

In the time of King Karlmann [r. 876-880] there was a sheriff in the Norican country, Sigihard, by name, who held the royal market at the trading sites on the river Sempt, whence the very same name of that place is derived. This Sigihard seeking the nearby woods in the autumn time in order to hunt, there in the southern part came upon an exceptional wild boar of unaccustomed size lurking between a sandstone outcropping and a linden tree, which, although driven away, returned there by night for some days and could not be taken. Finally, fleeing from the district it mocked all hope of their effort. Although they themselves were saying this was all an illusion, still they told it far and wide as a wonder, and a well-known religious cleric, Chounrad of Höwen (which is a fortress near the Bodensee) hearing the tale rumored about, charged Sigihard thus: "Order the place from which the remarkable boar lurking between the outcrop and the linden was flushed with such difficulty to be cleared, for by a divine manifestation I foretell that place to be raised up for divine service and to be occupied by servants of God who shall expel the Satan who wounds people with poisonous tooth. If you should erect a church, construct it separately in a pure place according to the custom of the ancients, who decreed that it was not good religious practice to frequent a church near a pagan place. If means permit, build walls, for, as God applied a scourge to the realm of the patricians Ermanric and Egidius, that is Attila the king of the Huns, so also shall he strike the present generation with a scourge to drive out sins." At the same time, some men coming from the city of Strassburg brought back a like prophecy for raising up the place which had been received from Gebehard, a hermit there. As a sign of believing these things, he [Sigihard] ordered all the trees in the grove to be cut down, which took place under his nephew, Oadalrich, during a heavy snowstorm. Thereafter, with that same place completely cleared and a stronghold which is called the 'Ebersberg' constructed of logs and fortified with pickets of intertwined branches, Arnolf the king, son of Karlmann, because he was a kinsman, enriching Sigihard with many properties, as an addition to the new fortress granted him three holdings in the vill of Kaging and three in the vill of Ötting with all things pertaining to them, validating the conveyanace by witness of the royal seal affixed [896].

In the year of the Lord's incarnation 906 Sigihard dying left the place Ebersberg to his son Ratold who was very active in both divine and secular matters for which reason the Emperor committed the Carinthian March to his protection. He [Ratold] remembering Chuonrad's prophecy expanded the immediate surroundings of the fort and completed the place at great expense. He begat Eberhard, Adalpero and Willibirg. Dying he left Ebersberg to Eberhard and was buried at Salzburg in the church of St Amand in the west corner which overflowed with the bodies of holy men.

At this time when the Huns, also known as Hungarians, were devastating the eastern boundaries, Eberhard undertook to encircle the fort with a wall and expand the ditches. But, on a certain night as he slept, he was awakened by a cock crowing. Falling asleep again he conceived himself to be walking about within the fort together with a crowd of knights and ministerials, showing to his workmen how he wanted the towers and workshops to be constructed in each place. The cock which had awakened him was changed into the form of a poor man who claimed to be a shepherd from the east and said to him: "The fort which you are building lies open to the snares of enemies if you do not build within it a dwelling place where watch may be kept over it. But if you will give to me incense, wine and oil, I shall undertake the obligations of safekeeping so that you yourself and those who with you provide these things to me shall suffer harm from no one [?]". While still alarmed by these things in the dreams that he should assign watchmen by turns to the stronghold and then erect a dwelling with materials for the watch procured from afar, and at great expense acquire incense together with wine and oil with which the vigil might be kept, wearily he kept the watch sweating and trembling. Concerned lest the dream presage something evil, after calling together Hunfrid his clerk and wise laymen, he told them the dream. But each offered his own conjectures according to how it seemed to him, and they failed to please his mind. Hunfrid then said: "The cock which is hatched from the mother's egg so that as night recedes he might announce the approach of day, in many places in the Scriptures signifies Jesus born of Mary who commands men to avoid the shadows, that is, evil works, and desire the day, that is, good works. He was destitute and poor in this world just as: 'Foxes have their holes …' [Matthew 8:20]. He is the shepherd according to Ezechial: 'As the shepherd searches …' [Ezechial 34:12], and he himself says: 'I am the good shepherd …' [John 10:11]. The Christians of the east, as the prophet testifies

[Zechariah 6:12] have their name from him whose name is Oriens and are called Orientals. And the Psalmist also testifies that the city in which watch is not kept is open to enemies, saying: 'Unless the Lord keeps watch ...' [Psalm 127:1]. Moreover, the incense which is burned therein signifies the right faith and devotion of the prayer: 'May my prayer like incense ...' [Psalm 141:2]. Also the Apocalypse: 'The prayers of the saints ...' [Revelations 5:8]. Wine signifies the bitterness of penitence: 'You have poured out for us the wine of remorse ...' [Vulgate Psalm 59:5]. Oil, which expels fatigue and provides light, signifies good works whence the maidens lacking in oil were shut out of the kingdom of heaven." After hearing this, Eberhard said: "Even if a thousand conjectures could be offered to me concerning this dream, still I would account all of them as nothing in comparison with this one which is recounted from the Holy Scriptures. Thus, in order that God might overlook my sins and deign to grant me heavenly grace, I now pray him to increase in me by good works right faith and remorse of heart. And if he should deign to prolong my life until I may build him a visible temple, I shall provide incense, wine and oil for its service." And on the following day he placed three stones upon the sandstone outcropping in the place where he intended to lay the eastern foundation. But Hunfrid told him that the house of God should rather be laid upon solid stone than be founded upon sand: "Remove the sandstone and cast down the linden tree which the common people revere as holy." After they had been removed according to his dictates, a church was built in the form of a cross, 50 feet in width and 80 feet in length, and in the intervening eight days all the masonry work was completed, which number, as Hunfrid demonstrated, contained not a few mysteries in both the Old and the New Law. A portable altar of consecrated marble containing the relics of St Sebastian was placed upon the main altar in whose name he [Eberhard] gave: for the service of God a tenement at Regensburg on the market; to buy incense four yokes of vineyards in Aschach-Winchil; Kaps; a place which is called "at Sempt"; Klettheim; two churches endowed with tithes at Tegernbach and Zorneding, and also the tithe of the hunt and of felling trees in the woods there. He also intended to give Aham, but he did not have the consent of his brother [Adalpero]. He appointed Hunfrid as head of the clerks assembled there [934]...

EXHIBIT II.5: GENEALOGY of the EBERSBERGERS

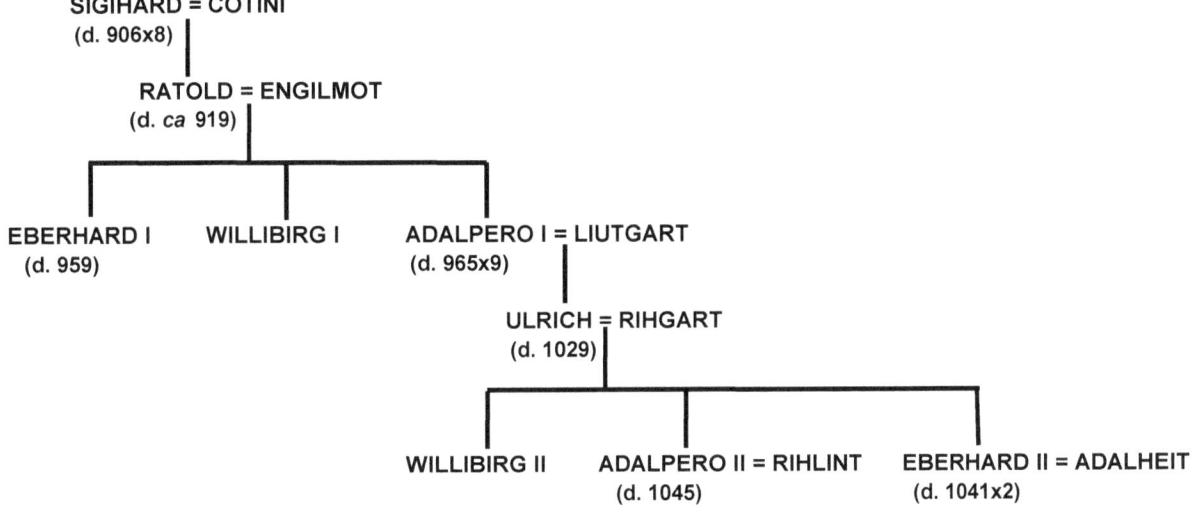

www.ingramcontent.com/pod-product-compliance
Ingram Content Group UK Ltd.
Pitfield, Milton Keynes, MK11 3LW, UK
UKHW061213180426
11947UKWH00029B/2028